AND THE
WINNER IS...

MARY B. GREBLA

AND THE WINNER IS...

TATE PUBLISHING
AND ENTERPRISES, LLC

Published by Tate Publishing & Enterprises, LLC
127 E. Trade Center Terrace | Mustang, Oklahoma 73064 USA
1.888.361.9473 | www.tatepublishing.com

Tate Publishing is committed to excellence in the publishing industry. The company reflects the philosophy established by the founders, based on Psalm 68:11,
"The Lord gave the word and great was the company of those who published it."

Book design copyright © 2015 by Tate Publishing, LLC. All rights reserved.
Cover design by Joana Quilantang
Interior design by Richell Balansag

Published in the United States of America

ISBN: 978-1-68207-083-3
Biography & Autobiography / Personal Memoirs
15.07.09

Foreword

You know, as a parent, that you would take all the knowledge that you have and give it to your children so that they do not have to go through what you have gone through. I would never want one of my children to go through any of the suffering that I have, but what I do want is for them to know my Jesus as I do. I have spent my entire life in a very special relationship with the King of kings, and the Lord of lords! So I want to first of all dedicate this book to my very best friend of my entire life, and that has been Jesus Christ, my Lord and Savior. He has been with me every second, every step of the way. He has seen my joy, wiped my tears many times, but most of all, He has never left my side and just watch what He does for me throughout my life. You can't ask for a greater friend on this side of heaven and the other…amen!

I had another best friend to which I want to dedicate this book to, that is my husband Bob. This is the angel that the Lord Jesus gave me very early on in my life at the age of fourteen to protect and help me. I feel like, if Jesus could not be physically by my side, He sent an angel for replacement! Just watch and read, you will see…

5

My entire life can be written into a book. There has been so many things in which the Lord has done, and then Satan has come in and has stolen or caused to crash, made to stumble, or whatever the event has been throughout my life, he was there to cause strife or he has just been flat-out contemptuous. Just the same as he does in every other Christian's life. God warns us of this in His Word when He tells us that Satan goes around as a roaring lion looking for whom he can devour. It took me over forty-five years of my life to find out just how much!!

> *Be sober, be vigilant; because your adversary the*
> *devil walks about like a roaring lion,*
> *seeking whom he may devour.*
>
> —1 Peter 5:8

But it is by the power of our testimonies that the power and authority of the Lord Jesus Christ shall go forth in all that we do!!!

Here is my testimony for the Lord Jesus Christ…

Quotes from the Lord

These are revelations from the Lord that I have heard over the years, and I have compiled on to one page. There are more, but these are the majors.

Pray for the SWAY.

Stop adjusting God's Word to fit your life.
Start adjusting your life to fit God's Word.

I want my women on fire for Christ.

You could wake up and there may not be a tomorrow as you remember your yesterday to be.

(March 2015)

This is one that the Lord spoke as I was writing this book; you will find it toward the end of the book. Believe me, it took me back too! I did not even know I had written it and had to go back to read what I wrote.

Our Lord is coming for His Bride, and we are now at the finish line in this race for our Lord Jesus Christ. So we need to be an army, geared up, marching and ready to defeat all enemies to get to the finish line that is directly ahead. (12/24/14)

1

My Very First Miracle
Jesus Starts with a Bang

My walk with the Lord began at the age of ten. Up until that time, we had a very rough time of it. We had a very young mother whom had been severely abused by an alcoholic husband, and we had come under his wrath a time or two, and even though the youngest of my siblings was yet just a baby, this had not mattered at all to him through his alcoholic haze and rage. All of this had left its scars on all of us in one way or another. The last time I ever saw my real father when he lived with us was at the age of five. I remember the day very well. My very pretty and young mother was sitting in the yard on a fence, watching my three-year-old sister Thelma and my infant sister Debra in the yard. He came up to her and drew a knife to her throat and was going to slice her throat. I ran to a neighbor's home to call the police on my own father. They were there rather quickly, and they took him away. I remember them placing him in the car that day. It is strange the pictures that remain with you no matter how old you get. That is one that I will never forget.

We soon moved away to another state, and I began to go to school for the very first time. Wow, that truly was a long time ago. I do believe I am getting old! I can remember the desks that were bolted to the floor and the principal that would come over the loudspeaker every single morning, and he would say a prayer every morning to begin the day. Then we would place our hand over our heart and we would pledge allegiance to the American flag of the United States of America, one nation under God! Then we would sing "God Bless America" in the one school I attended. Someone please tell me what happened to all of this?

Do you know, someone even reminded me the other day that we even had prayer right before we were let out to go to lunch! They blessed the lunch! This was not just in the Christian schools, guys; this was in all the schools across the United States of America. We used to be a united country that was a blessed country under the sovereign hand of an Almighty God because our leaders believed that only by placing God first could a country survive and go forward. Even Congress had a chaplain, and you would not see Congress begin without the chaplain there to say a prayer to begin their day. Go ahead go back and look at the archives! I dare anyone to go research history. Then what (or should I say who) happened. Oops, I got off on a soap box. But all of this truly is all part of God's plan because the Lord is returning, and the downfall of the United States had to come. It is here, friends. It is going according to plan, and soon, oh very soon, the Antichrist shall arise, and if you are still here with him, then you had better be looking for ways to hide. If you are a Tribulation Saint, you will be doing this the hard way. Most will lose their heads during this period. (You need to be praying to be out of here on the first boatload!) All right, I will get back to my testimony…

So as we moved around a bit in these few years, my mom was now trying to raise three very young girls on her own. Now remember, these days were very different than they are today. It was a very hard thing to do for a single woman to raise three very young children and try to work also. But one way or another, we always seemed to survive, and we always seemed to have something to eat even if it was not much. But the Lord always provided something. We eventually moved to a small town in New Jersey and settled there. I began school and began to meet friends.

For the first few years, my mom would get all three of us girls up on a Sunday morning when she was not working and she would dress us up, sometimes in matching dresses if they were available, and we would walk down to a large Baptist Church that was about seven or eight blocks down the road. To me, who was at that time between six to eight years old, it felt like it was about twenty blocks. One thing that I did not know, nor find out until over eight to nine years later, was that at the time we were attending this church on a regular basis, my future husband was also attending this church. He was even baptized one Sunday (so my mom says) while we were attending this church. It was about eight to nine years later that we got married in this very same church. We will come back to this…

Then as we began to get a little older, my mom began to work a little more, and she also began to have more of her own life, and she would go out with her own friends more and more. We spent a lot of time with sitters in those days. Church became rare occasions. Then I met neighbors who lived just a few doors down, and she was also a single mom with a large family of six children. Some were older and already gone from the home, but there were still three of her children who went to church all the time. One of her daughters was around my age.

This family became like my second family. Lois was the mom's name, and I cannot wait to give her the biggest hug when we all get to eternity. She loved the Lord so much, and she made sure that her children were at church all the time and for almost every event and function. If the doors were open, she and her family were through them. Thank you, Lord, for a dedicated mom. I began going with her family and became one of her family in everything that she did. Just about every time her car left for church, I was in it. We went to everything from nursing home ministries to and including tent revivals. Oh, how powerful the **Shekinah Glory** is when it is inside a tent!

We were going to an Assembly of God Church in Flemington, New Jersey, at this time. I went with them for almost two years, I believe it was. It was not just Sunday mornings either. It seemed like we were always at a church function or doing something with the church. Many Sundays I remained with the pastor's family until Lois came back that evening. Serving the Lord was a very large part of that church at that time. I knew the Lord and about Him from many years of Sunday school and church. I had heard about Jesus since I could remember. It felt like I had known about Him just about all my life. Now I know this is how every child should be brought up.

Even though I truly thought I already loved the Lord Jesus, it was at the age of ten, and in one Sunday night's service when miracle number 1 happened. This young girl must have been paying attention to the pastor's words this night. For when he called for the altar call and asked for those who wanted to give their hearts to Jesus to come and kneel at the altar, I got up out of my seat and I went to the altar. What happened next has been engraved upon my memory. I have not forgotten one moment of that night.

I remember this night as if it were yesterday, and it happened over forty-five years ago. If you are looking at the front of the church and the altar is across the front with the pulpit in the center, I knelt down on the right hand side of the altar. I began praying for Jesus to come into my heart and save me from my sins as a ten-year-old would do...

That was the last thing that I remember in the natural world. What happened next has been my testimony for forty-five years. I can tell you that many people, including pastors, do not believe that such a thing can happen. They give it any other explanation except what it actually was...

It was a *very real* meeting with the Lord Jesus Christ, My Savior, My Redeemer, My Everything! He was standing there with His arms outstretched to me, and then I remember being at His feet. How long I was with Jesus, I could not tell you. What we spoke about I could not tell you. From the time I knelt down at the right side of the altar and my encounter with Jesus began, somewhere in here, I began speaking in tongues. I do not know at what point someone physically moved me, but I know I was slain in the Spirit totally while I was with Jesus. They moved me from the right side of the altar to the left side of the altar. I did not remember any of this. I was still with Jesus, and we were having a conversation.

As I was coming back to the church from my meeting with Jesus, I can tell you that this ten-year-old child was shaken to the core of her bones. As I woke up, I was laying flat up, on top of the left side of the altar, still speaking in tongues. The lights had been all turned down low except the altar lights and the back door. Most of the church had left except some very strong praying people, who were all sort of sitting around the front of the altar where I was, and they were all just praying. Well, as I said, I was shaken to the core. I knew I had just met Jesus, and everyone was looking at me and everyone was crying…even myself. I jumped up off that altar where I was lying, and I ran to Lois, who was sitting right in the front row now, and she was praying. I jumped up in her lap, and we both just cried as she held me and just rocked me, just as if I was a small child.

After a few minutes as I calmed down a bit, as we were both crying, I asked, "What happened?" I then told Lois and those who were sitting there near me, like the Pastor Zabriski, that I just saw Jesus. I have never forgotten Lois's next words.

She said, "Honey, you have just been saved in the mightiest way." It was not until I was a little older and could understand more of the things of God that I totally understood what had happened that night. All I knew at the age of ten was that I had met Jesus, and that I knew that Jesus was very, very real. There has never been anything or anyone that could ever shake my faith in the Lord, for I not only met Him, I spent time with Him, and I sat at His feet as He spoke with me. Boy, I cannot wait until I get to see Him again and ask Him what it was that He said to me that day so long ago.

I want to take the time to add here, please do not think for one minute that I consider myself better than anyone else that has not had an experience like this. If I am honest with myself, I feel quite the opposite. I feel wonderfully honored and blessed, but I know Him to have seen and been with Him. It is those of you who have believed in our Lord Jesus without any special help or visits from the Lord, and it is by your faith alone that you believe in Him and His love for you that Jesus Himself said was blessed. Look what Jesus said to Thomas when Thomas needed the proof that it was truly Jesus:

> *Jesus said to him, "Thomas, because you have seen Me, you have believed. Blessed are those who have not seen and yet have believed." (John 20:29)*

So for people like myself who have had these special encounters with the Lord, this does not make us any better than the next person. The only advantage that I think I have is that my faith in the Lord is totally unshakeable. No matter who you are, if you do not believe that the Lord Jesus Christ is who He says He is and you do not believe that the gifts of the Holy Spirit are real, I just feel very sorry for you. For not believing in the Lord Jesus, you get to spend all of eternity in a Lake of Fire in a Literal Hell. For Christians and others who do not believe that the gifts of the Holy Spirit are not real, then all you do is to rob yourself of parts of the most intimate moments that could be yours with the Lord now while you are still here. But it is only because these two things are very real that Satan is out there in this world doing all the damage that he possibly can to destroy people's belief in both.

But guess what? I peeked at the end of the book. Jesus wins!!!!!! Those who have chosen to believe the world and not to believe in the Lord Jesus shall have the chance to spend all eternity in Hell with Satan because no matter what comes from the evil one, it shall not last and our Lord Jesus Christ shall triumph over all! So I pray that if Jesus calls you to Himself by the Holy Spirit, please respond and listen. For every single person on earth shall have this chance and they shall be able to accept or reject the calling of the Holy Spirit. Not one person will be able to stand in front of the Lord Jesus at Judgment and say, "But I had no idea!"

No one can come to Me unless the Father who sent Me draws him; and I will raise him up at the last day.

(John 6:44)

Therefore, as the Holy Spirit says: "Today, if you will hear His voice, Do not harden your hearts as in the rebellion, In the day of trial in the wilderness, Where your fathers tested Me, tried Me,

And saw My works forty years. Therefore I was angry with that generation, And said, 'They always go astray in their heart, And they have not known My ways.' So I swore in My wrath, 'They shall not enter My rest.'"

Beware, brethren, lest there be in any of you an evil heart of unbelief in departing from the living God; but exhort one another daily, while it is called "Today," lest any of you be hardened through the deceitfulness of sin. For we have become partakers of Christ if we hold the beginning of our confidence steadfast to the end, while it is said: "Today, if you will hear His voice, Do not harden your hearts as in the rebellion."

(Hebrews 3:7–15)

2

The Battle Begins

I got to enjoy my newfound love and joy very briefly. Oh, how happy I was in those days. I could not wait to be at church, and I lived for Sundays and Wednesdays or any time that we could go back to the House of the Living God. I immediately wanted to be baptized, and I was. Oh, what a joy that was. Then the bottom fell out of my world. We moved away, and then Lois and her family moved out of the area. I remember once or twice my mom taking me to church at my church, but it was now so far away that we just did not go anymore.

I remember trying many churches close by that maybe my mom could take me to, but the one that was the closest just did not seem the same, so I asked not to go back. Eventually, they were too busy or working and I could not get to church. It was around this time that my mom had my new baby sister, Barbara. Now there were four girls to raise, and our family was changing daily. So if I wanted to go to church, I had to walk to ones close by. As we lived on a busy highway at the time and I was still a young girl, this was not a good idea.

It was a short two years after my meeting with the Lord that the course of my life drastically began to change. Now, forty-three years later and many talks with the Lord recently, the entire picture of what has taken place over all of these years has become very clear. For so very long, it has been the enemy that has blinded me to the truth, and it was the enemy that took me down every time to kill and destroy what the Lord had set in motion. I now truly know and believe that Satan was watching that day when a ten-year-old girl met Jesus. He knew there was a path coming, and he has done everything in his power to stop me along the way. I believe that he heard what was said, even though I did not remember. But since that day, he has done all that he could to stop my forward progress. Hence this book! But praise be to the Lord Most High that He is truly more powerful, more of everything! But most of all, His Word has come to pass time and time again in my life, but it was not until this past two years that I saw the full scope of my life revealed to me. For He tells us right from the start that once we belong to Him, He will never leave us or forsake us! These are not my words, they belong to the Lord!

> *Be strong and of good courage, do not fear nor be afraid of them; for the Lord your God, He is the One who goes with you. He will not leave you nor forsake you. (Deuteronomy 31:6)*

For those of you who like the New Testament...

> *For I am convinced that neither death nor life, neither angels nor demons, neither the present nor the future, nor any powers, neither height nor depth, nor anything else in all creation, will be able to separate us from the love of God that is in Christ Jesus our Lord. (Romans 8:38–39)*

> *Let your conduct be without covetousness; be content with such things as you have. For He Himself has said, "I will never leave you nor forsake you." (Hebrews 13:5)*

Ding-Ding...Round 1
Divine Intervention!
Miracle #2

One day, during a summer break from school, I was walking to the store for something that my uncle wanted. During those days, leg power was the most popular form of transportation. It was probably about one and a half to two miles each way. While I was almost home, it began to rain. I was at the bottom of an exit ramp; as I was walking along a main road, the car coming down the ramp could not stop for the oncoming traffic and ran right into me. The impact of the car tossed me to the side of the road. As I lay there on the ground, two older people got out of their car to make sure that I was all right. I then tried to get up from the ground, and even though hurting, I told them I could walk and was okay. They got back in their car and left. I did not realize it at the time, but they should have taken me home regardless. But to this day, I am glad that the Lord had His hand in all of that, for they were an elderly couple, and they were so shaken. I know they should have stayed, but I believe the enemy meant it all for evil, especially after what happened when I got home. I could see my house from where I was, and I just needed to get home where I knew my mom was. I pointed to my home and told them that I lived right there. I believe that it was sheer adrenalin from the Lord that carried me home.

Number 1, I thank the Lord that the impact did not throw me out into the middle of the road, but it threw me off to the side of the road. Number 2, I thank the Lord for His strength, His courage, and His stamina. Number 3, I believe that the Lord had His hand between that car and myself, as it should have been much worse than it was! Here is where Miracle #2 and my Divine Intervention comes in…It is only now that I know because of all that the Lord has shown to me, that it was right here that the enemy began to try and take my life. He wanted me stopped, and he wanted me stopped permanently. But Jesus had other plans for my life…

When I walked in the back door that day and told my Mom what had happened, I lost all my adrenalin and then

I felt every bit of what happened. They immediately took me to the hospital where I spent quite a bit of time due to the injury to my back. The one I felt most sorry for though was my uncle, who sent me to the store that day. I loved him so much, yet I do not ever think he forgave himself for sending me. I pray that he knows now that it was not his fault, but all in the plans of Satan to remove one more weapon against himself.

This injury was to cause the rest of my testimony which comes next. This testimony will last the course of the next forty years. So in hindsight, our enemy is quite dumb if he thinks that he can get one over on the Lord. For all it has done over all of these years is to bring more and more glory to the name above all names…Jesus!

> **Be sober, be vigilant; because your adversary the devil walks about like a roaring lion, seeking whom he may devour. (1 Peter 5:8)**

Ding!!! Ding!!!!! Satan loses the round!

3

God Sends an Angel
Miracle #3

It was a short two years later after having my automobile accident that I was getting very discouraged with not being able to attend church anymore, and I would have to stay home all the time and take care of my small sisters while my mom worked. It was then that I met a young man that happened to live right next door. Yes, I was only fourteen years old and very young. In those days, being young was not the same as it is today. I was a very mature fourteen from raising my sisters while my mom had to work. We were raised very differently in those days, at least I was. From the day that I met my future husband Bob, I said, "God has sent me an angel." He was one of the nicest, kindest, most gentlest human beings I had ever encountered in my young life. If I said that statement once, I said it a hundred times over the years…

Now many people right here are going to be saying, "It was not Satan who did this!" Well, after everything that comes next, I know better. It was the earlier churches and teachings that I heard in my life (and not my first home church either!) that taught me that if I did something wrong, it was going to be God Himself that punished me. So from a very young age, every time something drastic happened, I thought I was getting punished. For I knew that I was a Christian, and I knew that I belonged to Jesus, so I figured that every time I did something wrong, I was being punished. Oh, how very wrong I was! Does God chastise his children? You bet He does. He will bring you to where He wants you by His means. But He will never ever hurt you. God will bring about His discipline using the Holy Spirit, and you will know that it is the Lord when He is through with you. In Hebrews 12, it tells us all about the Lord's discipline of His children. Here is a small part. But do yourself a favor and read the whole text to receive the entire glory of God's Word.

> *And you have forgotten the exhortation which speaks to you as to sons: "My son, do not despise the chastening of the Lord, Nor be discouraged when you are rebuked by Him; For whom the Lord loves He chastens, And scourges every son whom He receives. (Hebrews 12:5, 6)*

God is our Heavenly Father, and as such, we need to be placing Him first and foremost in our lives. He is a very jealous God and wants nothing to take His children away from Him. But He will also allow His children to walk off and do their own thing. But He is always standing by to catch us. Now I believe that there is scripture that says God can take us home, but that is much deeper than this short story. But it is my heartfelt belief that nothing and no one (including yourself) can take you from the hand of God. Since this is my book and my story, I can relate my own beliefs and how strongly I stand on them. This is why Jesus took the time to teach the parable of the prodigal son. This is what some of us are in our lives at one point or another. We try to do things our own way and then the Lord says, "No, son, come home to me…"

The Parable of the Lost Son

Then He said: "A certain man had two sons. And the younger of them said to his father, 'Father, give me the portion of goods that falls to me.' So he divided to them his livelihood. And not many days after, the younger son gathered all together, journeyed to a far country, and there wasted his possessions with prodigal living. But when he had spent all, there arose a severe famine in that land, and he began to be in want. Then he went and joined himself to a citizen of that country, and he sent him into his fields to feed swine. And he would gladly have filled his stomach with the pods that the swine ate, and no one gave him anything.

"But when he came to himself, he said, 'How many of my father's hired servants have bread enough and to spare, and I perish with hunger! I will arise and go to my father, and will say to him, "Father, I have sinned against heaven and before you, and I am no longer worthy to be called your son. Make me like one of your hired servants."'"

"And he arose and came to his father. But when he was still a great way off, his father saw him and had compassion, and ran and fell on his neck and kissed him. And the son said to him, 'Father, I have sinned against heaven and in your sight, and am no longer worthy to be called your son.'

"But the father said to his servants, 'Bring out the best robe and put it on him, and put a ring on his hand and sandals on his feet. And bring the fatted calf here and kill it, and let us eat and be merry; for this my son was dead and is alive again; he was lost and is found.' And they began to be merry.

"Now his older son was in the field. And as he came and drew near to the house, he heard music and dancing. So he called one of the servants and asked what these things meant. And he said to him, 'Your brother has come, and because he has received him safe and sound, your father has killed the fatted calf.'

"But he was angry and would not go in. Therefore his father came out and pleaded with him. So he answered and said to his father, 'Lo, these many years I have been serving you; I never transgressed your commandment at any time; and yet you never gave me a young goat, that I might make merry with my friends. But as soon as this son of yours came, who has devoured your livelihood with harlots, you killed the fatted calf for him.'

"And he said to him, 'Son, you are always with me, and all that I have is yours. It was right that we should make merry and be glad, for your brother was dead and is alive again, and was lost and is found.'"

(Luke 15:11–32)

Just as this father was waiting with open arms, so is our Heavenly Father waiting for us with open arms. He will never come to hurt us or inflict injury on us. That is like saying your own dad would want to purposely hurt you for anything. Does our natural dad get mad and punish us when we do wrong? They most certainly do (or at least they should be). But almost every dad has so much love for their children that even though they will give them a reprimand or punishment to show them the correct behavior in life, our Heavenly Father does the very same thing, but will never hurt us. God loves us with an unconditional love, and there is nothing that he would not do for us or give us if we just asked Him with a correct heart and motives. But most do not ask, for they do not believe that our Lord is that powerful to provide what they would want or need in their lives. Oh, my friends, what you deprive yourselves of. A relationship with the Lord of lords and King of kings that says, "He loves me to the utmost!"

> *You lust and do not have. You murder and covet and cannot obtain. You fight and war. Yet you do not have because you do not ask. You ask and do not receive, because you ask amiss, that you may spend it on your pleasures. (James 4:3)*

I say all of this because in many ways, I became the prodigal son of our Lord. Yes, me, the one who sat at His feet, the one who saw Him, the one who sat and spoke with him for an unspecified amount of time. Yet I still became more concerned with the things in this life and began to walk in the world more and more. I could no longer go to church with Lois and her family as they had moved away from the area, and I could no longer go with them. I could not find a local church that was anywhere near what I had come out of, so nothing was the same. When I say anywhere near, I mean a full Holy Spirit–filled, Bible-believing, fully gifted church. In today's language, they call these Pentecostal churches. When you are born in these churches, nothing else will fill your spirit and soul the same as a good old-fashioned Pentecostal church. God keep them going until you call us home! I know for myself, I feel empty when I leave a church that is not filled with the Full Spirit of the Holy Ghost. It is like going to dinner at a restaurant and still leaving completely hungry.

So I pulled out of church at the age of fourteen when I met Bob. As I said earlier, yes, I was very young, but extremely mature for my age. I would be going to school every day and then coming right home to care for my sisters until my mom would get home from work. Bob was the greatest, he actually helped me with my three sisters. My sister Barbara was only a baby at the time, and he would tend to her just as if she was his own. He was just amazing. He loved children, and he would sit for hours and play with Barbara Lee. He just loved her, and she loved him. Matter of fact, I never met a child or animal, or even an adult for that matter, that did not love Bob. Even my mom loved and defended this man. He became the best friend of my new stepdad, and they did everything together. I told you it was crazy. Everyone loved Bob. Like I said, "God sent me an angel." You just could find no wrong in the man. By the time I was one day shy of the age of sixteen, we were getting married in the Baptist church that we both attended when we were both very young children. No, I was not pregnant! I just want to make that disclaimer because it is usually the first thing people say. "Were you pregnant?" No, I was not, matter of fact, I did not have my first child until the age of twenty. I was just a very mature young lady and I married very, very young.

Miracle #4

As I said, we began having children when I was twenty years old. This was almost one year to the day that the doctors told me that I would *never* have *any* children. We had been trying now for three years and were not having any success. Bob loved children so much, and I did so want to give him his own children. Finally, we began with the medical testing to find out why I could not get pregnant. The doctors told us that we would never be able to have any children between us due to several reasons. After this very devastating blow, we now had given up *all* hope of having children and I was moving forward with schooling, when along came our first miracle child...Jennifer. We were so happy and fulfilled with the gift that the Lord had given us and we did not think that there would ever be another child for us. So we were quite content with our happy little family. But God had other plans...

Miracle #5

About five years later, we had moved to Washington, New Jersey. At the time, I had been attending the Washington Assembly of God Church. At this time, the church was in the middle of quite a population explosion. At the time, we had a most precious man of God as our pastor, a Reverend Gerald Scott Sr. Since these days, he has gone on to be with the Lord, and his son has stepped into his place, but I can still hear his words in our church during one late spring morning during 1984. He said, "Ladies, be careful, there are seeds of the Lord on these seats," and he was speaking of all the women in the church that were at that moment pregnant (which were *many*). It was not but a short month or so later that I became pregnant with our next miraculous gift, miracle #5. We called him Jeffrey, which meant "gift from God," and Scott for Pastor Scott, who prophesied his arrival. To this day, regardless of which direction Jeffrey goes or what he does, I know that this boy has a gift from the Lord, and the Lord God has a purpose and a direction in which Jeffrey cannot and will not be able turn away from. The Lord shall call his name, and he shall answer him to the mission in which the Lord has called him to do. I just pray the Lord shall guide him along this path until the mission the Lord has shall be fulfilled.

Both of our children have been precious gifts from the Lord God, and we have been most grateful and love them with a love that exceeds all that even we can comprehend. The love in which we have for our children has given us the comprehension of the love in which the Father has for us, with one exception. We have taught our children that our love for them is unconditional, just as the Father's love for us is unconditional. There is nothing that they can do to earn, warrant, deserve, nor can they lose that love. This is how God the Father is with us, *except* His is Love is infinitely more deeper and shall be eternally never-ending.

We can not even fathom the depths nor the heights or the realm of His love for us. We are only on a human level. He is on an Almighty Father, Alpha, Omega, the Great I Am level!!!! And just think, this is your Father...Wow!!!

The miracles of the Lord have been tremendous to this young girl so far. But this is only a drop in the bucket for what is coming. The enemy thinks that he can stop the will of the Almighty God by taking down someone because they do not know God's Word. Boy, it has been a while since he spent some time around the Almighty God, hasn't it? Our Lord is mighty and He has an agenda that will not be destroyed!!!

God Never Lets Go…

As the years passed, due to my spinal injury from the accident, I ended up with many, many medical problems. My spinal column was getting continually worse and creating many other problems along the way. I was now back in church and I was serving the Lord, as I could now drive myself. But I also was coming and going because I would end up having problems with alcohol mostly in the spring after dealing with a long winter and pain. It would only last for a few months and then it would end until the fall and the cold months began again. I was now bipolar, at least this was the label they placed on it. I had a lot of "labels" back in the early '80s. I had chronic pain syndrome and fibromyalgia too . I know this may be hard for many to understand, but I guess for many years, I was very stubborn, and I just was not going to give in to what was going on. I did not go to the doctors for all of my maladies. I just endured them and got through them the best I could. I only went when I absolutely had to. I am not a doctors person, unless they make me go, or the pain is so bad that I cannot tolerate it anymore.

I knew that my pain was getting worse in my spine, and I knew that my body was getting worse. In 1981, when Jennifer was less than two years old, was the very first time that my spine locked up and went out for the very first time. That was about nine years after my accident. From that point on, it was all downhill. I had good points and that was usually the warm months. But when it turned cold, things got bad quickly. That was why in the spring, I had had enough and I usually turned to alcohol for relief. It was not every year, but it happened enough to be an issue. I did not take drugs, so I turned to alcohol for my relief. It did not take long to learn that alcohol dulled pain of all kind. So instead, I figured out that if I had a drink, it numbed the pain. I only found out too late that this was not the way to do it! (Now I know Jesus takes care of all pain! But I did not know then what I know now!) Eventually, I ended up a full-blown alcoholic by year sixteen of our marriage. But my God is still in the Miracle Business!

The Hand of God!!!
Miracles Uncounted!!!
Ding-Ding…Round 2!

Here is the next way that the enemy tried to destroy what God had put together. The first was when he tried to take me out at twelve years old. But now, the enemy tries to take out both me and my children together, but God had other plans. Watch this one! It was a late fall day, and my very young teenage sister Barbara, who had just gotten her driver's license, and her girl friend drove all the way up to the Poconos. She said, "Why don't you let me drive you to Mom's and then Bob can pick you all up from there? This way, I can show you how well I drive."

Well, she was so excited that I could not tell her no. Our son was about two and our daughter about seven. Barbara was almost seven months pregnant with her first child Danielle. As we all began our trip into New Jersey, there was construction at the bridge after the toll booth on Route 80 in New Jersey. There was a very nasty truck driver that began to play chicken with Barbara as everyone tried to funnel into one lane going across this bridge. Every time she would try to go and he waved her on, he would speed up and cut her off. Then he would wave her on again. It unnerved her. She finally got onto the bridge and began going down Route 80. She was in the farthest lane to the left coming up on her exit. I mentioned to her that she was going to have to take the exit coming up. So she placed on her blinker, and as I am a very experienced driver, so just on instinct, my head turned to the right. My head turned right and nothing was there. As she began to execute her turn to the right to get over into the middle lane, all of a sudden, the same truck that was nastily playing chicken with her at the bridge was right there, and he was almost ahead of her. She was going underneath the trailer of this tractor-trailer.

I began to scream first. As I did, Barbara's girl friend who had her head resting on the rear passenger window flew on top of my two children who were in the backseat that did not even have seat belts on, nor was Jeffrey in a car seat for they were not mandatory at that time. Children still sat up in back windows back then! Not mine, but I saw some do it. If she did not do that, at that split second, she would have been beheaded, for that is exactly where the wheels of the trailer came into the car. Exactly where her head was. I believe with all my heart that once again, she was an angel of the Lord, sent to save my children that day.

Now as that miracle is taking place in the backseat we have our own taking place in the front, for as we begin to go under the trailer of this truck, we were just bouncing down New Jersey Interstate Route 80, bouncing off the median, across three lanes of traffic, missing all three lanes of oncoming vehicles! Our marks are probably still there to this day on the median! I know they were the last time I looked! As I looked at Barbara, she had her arms up in the air and off the steering wheel, feet off the gas and the brakes, and she was screaming in shock. To my utter amazement, I can tell you that I felt hands on my shoulders holding me down in my seat! This is exactly what I told the officers at the hospital. They told us we should be dead and that someone must have been holding us in those seats! Praise you, Jesus, for your love and mercy!!!

Anyway, if that wasn't even miraculous enough, it just does not stop!!! As I looked at Barbara, she had absolutely no control of the car and we were bouncing all over Route 80. Even though I felt restrained at the shoulders, I took my left leg and my left arm and reached over and I turned off the ignition, and with my left leg, I slammed on the brakes and held them down until we came to a stop!!! I must tell you, this took all I had in strength. We came to a stop about one foot from the guardrail and going over a very steep precipice into the Delaware River.

The EMT workers were squeezing me out in this one foot section and trying to get me to stand up because I kept telling them I was all right. I knew I had just slammed on the brakes and I felt all right. As they stood me up, I went right to the ground, as my left foot Achilles tendon was severed. This is the same foot that had just slammed on the brake and kept it there to stop that car. No one knew how that occurred…I did!!!

Barbara who was seven months pregnant had a few cuts, but was fine and went on to have a normal childbirth with Danielle, two months later. Praise God. My children had some glass in their hair, but otherwise seemed to be fine. My daughter had one episode of her eyesight, but then the Lord made that well in a heartbeat. The girl who saved their lives was perfectly fine, and I suffered the Achilles tendon and was off my feet for about three months, and then my spinal injuries just began to escalate. But my spine was already on its way, so the injuries were minimal, and I thank God that I took the brunt of all that Satan tried to do to my family. For it was my poor husband that got the call that his whole family had just been in this horrific accident. Remember I said earlier that the Lord sent me an angel. I was not kidding. I said it from day 1. I am still saying this forty-two years later.

God sent us so many miracles that day, they were just too numerous to even count. The witnesses at the accident said that we should all be dead. The EMTs and the officers at the scene all said same thing. Even the policeman at the hospital had to admit that there had been Divine intervention that day. The car was totaled, all the windows out of it, yet we inside were well and intact. It was one of the most phenomenal things you would ever witness. Not too many people that drive under the trailer of a moving tractor-trailer can live to talk about it.

Ding-ding...end of round 2...satan, you lose!!!

5

Major Healing Miracle #1
The Sevenfold Miracles
Ding-Ding…Round 3

By year sixteen of our marriage, I was not on guard from the enemy and he had a heyday. Believe me, I know it now, that it was the enemy once more trying to destroy what God had put together.

I had had a long winter in the Poconos, and by the spring, I was telling my husband that I no longer wanted to be married because I was done. I did not want to put him through all that I was putting him through. I had thought long and hard about my decision before this because I had decided to leave my children with him. I know you are saying, "What mother can do this?" Answer? "A mother who loves her children with all her heart!"

You already know how I feel about Bob, and I was having problems dealing with the alcohol and the pain. I knew that Bob had the stable environment and that the children did not need to go through my problems. They were only nine and four at the time. I knew they were better off with him. So I allowed the enemy to convince me that this was the avenue that I must take, and I left my home. When I left, I was drinking very heavily to dull the pain, I was a full-blown anorexic and bulimic, I had just destroyed my marriage, and my life as I saw it was done. I had lost sight of everything at that point. But one thing I never lost sight of was Jesus. I still knew that I had Him by my side *always*. I just never had the comprehension as to the "why." The one thing that I have always believed all the way through this entire time was that this was my lot in life, and that because I did drink, that I was now being punished and I needed to pay for it. So I accepted it and allowed things to progress and get worse, thinking that I could not win. I did not know any better. I allowed the enemy to tell me that I needed to walk away from everything that God had put together. I am so glad that my God is greater!!!

I got myself a small home and I spent a lot of time alone with the Lord. It was only a few short months later as I sat in lunch with my girlfriend and she asked me what I was going to do because I was beside myself with loss and grief from all that was going on, I said to her (and I will never forget the words), "Only God can help me now." I was missing my children so badly that I just could not bear it anymore. I was even missing my husband, whom just a few short months earlier, the enemy had me believing that I did not love anymore. Well, this was about the beginning of September. It was by the end of September, which by the way was only a few short weeks, that I was moving back into my home with my husband and family. It was by October that I was healed, and I do mean *healed* from the alcoholism, I was *healed* from the anorexia and bulimia, I was *healed* from being bipolar, but the biggest healing of all was just about to take place within my marriage.

This one took a few months, but after a few months, Bob and I sat down one night and renewed our relationship to each other and before the Lord with an entirely new walk with Him, and let me just say, I love this walk so much more. It has been an entirely different life. I truly believe that the Lord placed a new heart in me for my husband, as I have had such a deeper love for him ever since the day I returned home at that point as I never had for him before. We have not only been husband and wife, we have been best friends, and it was in December of that year that Bob asked me once again to begin again, and we have never looked back. As we have the Lord as our captain of our ship who keeps us on a path, which goes on each day, this ship has been sailing a course that has been glory bound with the Lord at the helm, and we knew that no matter what the direction, all would be well. For those first years even though we both were in the church, it was not until we moved to North Carolina that Bob found out what a Spirit-filled Christian was all about. I will write about this later. Bob was great these first years, but oh boy, does he sure change when he meets the Holy Spirit face-to-face. I cannot wait to share this one.

As for my children, I cannot even begin to describe the joy that fills a mother's heart to be reunited with her children when she thinks that she will never have them in her life because of the choices that she has made. My children can never understand what I had to go through to get back to them, but I never wanted to leave them, but what I did, I did for them. I know this is going to be hard for so many to understand, but you would need to be in that position to actually understand it. But my life had become so bad, and I was believing the lies of an enemy that was from the very pits of hell itself. Once again, hindsight is 20/20, and if I had only known how to stand up within God's Word so much more and to be so much stronger way back then, I could have whipped the enemy then. But there was so much yet I needed to learn. My heart consisted of two things, my family and the Lord. They were both everything in the world to me. So when I lost my family and I cried out to the Lord, He heard my cries, and in my weakness and sickness, He saved me out of it and restored and healed me. The Lord who says that He will "never leave us nor forsake us" means every Word that He says…

> *Be strong and of good courage, do not fear nor be afraid of them; for the Lord your God, He is the One who goes with you. He will not leave you nor forsake you. (Deuteronomy 31:6)*

This is one of the reasons why I am such a firm believer in the fact that if you are a *true* (and I do mean *true*) child of God, that no matter where we are in or lives, that even in the depths of our trials, and no matter where we are, the Lord will reach in with His might and pull us out of the muck and the mire and save us even from ourselves! It is the enemy that entices us away into temptation and sin. Just as the enemy did with Adam and Eve. Absolutely nothing has changed since the creation of the earth. God says that too. I will not get too deep here, for many do not agree with me here. But if they lived it…they would believe it.

> *That which has been is what will be, That which is done is what will be done, And there is nothing new under the sun. Is there anything of which it may be said, "See, this is new"? It has already been in ancient times before us.*

> *(Ecclesiastes 1:9–10)*

So there surely was nothing new in my life here. The enemy had come in to take down a life that the Lord had put together. From an early age, I knew already that I belonged to the Lord Jesus, and apparently, so did the enemy!! I used alcohol for many years to numb the pain because I was not really a doctor person unless absolutely necessary. I did not do street drugs, and it seemed like the safest alternative. Yeah, right!! That was the biggest lie of the enemy going to date. So the enemy came in to lie, cheat, steal, and destroy. But the Lord stepped in and reversed all that the enemy had done to date. I call all of this my sevenfold miracles. The Lord came in to sweep up after the mess that the enemy had made of our home which was also the Lord's Home!!! Praise you, Lord! My life remains forever cleansed from all of these things, and I will forever praise Him!

Just a note here for the reader. Do you see how very easy it is to allow the enemy in when you think that you are living for the Lord with all of your heart? We did too. But it does not take much but an open crack in that armor, and the enemy will penetrate. It is so very important for all of us to wear the full armor of God every day in which our feet touch the floor.

The Lord says to be careful if you think you are standing firm…lest you fall. We need to be on our guards in these last hours because the enemy is roaming around searching out those whom he can devour and get off track. He wants nothing more than to make you fall! So stay in the ring. Stand up if you get knocked down. Get back up kicking and screaming! I will address this at the end of this book. But let me tell you, I got back up kicking and screaming!!! And praising God for the sevenfold miracles and the glory that just went forth!!!

Ding-ding…end of round 3, satan…you loser!

6

The Years of Unbelief
Ding-Ding…Round 4!

Let me just tell you that the enemy is never letting the grass grow under his feet before he is back at it to try and take me down again! It was in 1970 that I met the Lord Jesus face-to-face. The enemy saw that! It was in 1972 when I was hit by the car. Just less than two short years later. My sevenfold miracles were in 1991. It was in 1993 when I had to totally go out of work for the very last time because my pain was very bad that I was now in tears on a daily basis. I actually picked up the phone and told a doctor if he did not help me, I was going home to the Lord that day because I could not bear the pain anymore. He pulled me right into the office that day. Thank the Lord for that started some help for the following year, for some semi-relief, but he tried to get me some surgery, but even this doctor could not find anyone to do surgery on a woman so young! They all kept saying I was "too young too have such bad back problems." I kept saying, "You wanna bet!" I even had one say it was all in my head. When this doctor sent his bill to me, I sent it back unpaid and wrote on it: "This bill is all in your head!" I prayed to the Lord, "Forgive me, Lord, for this, but, Lord, I will not pay for Satan's antics." I never got another bill from that doctor again!

From 1993 to late 1997, I battled doctors and basically battled for my life. I was getting very, very bad in both pain and being able to walk and move. I kept trying to get doctors to correctly diagnose me. I was diagnosed with everything from Lyme disease to chronic pain syndrome to fibromyalgia and was even told I was a drug addict. All I knew is that as the days passed, I was going downhill, and I could not get anyone to believe that it was my spine. I kept telling them that I was hit by a car at the age of twelve and that I had a bad spine, but they said, "No, you are too young to have a bad spine." I was like…yikes! Even friends and family were beginning to look at me like "What is wrong with her? She is too young to have so many problems. She is just a complainer." I even had much loved friends walk away because they said they could not handle my being so ill. I have news for everyone. I did not enjoy it either! Oh, I tried so hard to get someone to believe the pain that I was having. My favorite I think was the entire year that my family doctor kept treating me for Lyme disease even though test after test kept coming back negative! So for an entire year, I took antibiotics.

In late 1997, I had what was almost like a stroke, and my left side was spasming. I went to the ER. The doctor in the ER called my family doctor, who had been treating me for this Lyme disease for the past year! And I had been taking penicillin for months on end now. He had taken multiple Lyme disease tests that came back negative (which by the way **each test** costs hundreds and hundreds of dollars). His response was…"Well, take the penicillin anyway, sometimes the results are wrong." He even sent me to a specialist with the same results! Well, when the ER doctor came back in, he said that my family doctor told him was that I was addicted to drugs. Now mind you, they had already drawn blood in the ER!!!

I said to him, "Absolutely not!! I take antibiotics that he is giving me for so called Lyme's disease. That is all I was taking!!" Not even a pain pill for the pain!!!"

I asked if anything else came up in the blood work, and he said, "Well…No…But…But…But…Your…Doctor… Says that you are addicted to drugs."

OH Garbage! In tears now, I walked out of there, never allowing him to finish his sentence. Still with the same spasming face and body.

Now the next day, I called to get into my dad's orthopedic surgeon's office for an emergency appointment. My dad's surgeon was not in, so I had to see an associate. When I got there and saw the associate doctor, he also left the room, and when he came back in, he said to me…and I do quote

…Mary, I want you to leave here and go directly to a rehab! I do not want you to even go home. I just spoke to your family doctor and he said you are addicted to drugs."

Well, now…I lost it, and so did my mom, who was with me. We were both crying! We could not believe what was happening! He turned around and walked out of the room before I could even say anything to him. I went to walk out of the room, and as I approached the front desk, they handed me a phone, and it was the rehab center for me to check in. I got on the phone with them and told them to forget it, I was not coming!!! And I walked out of that office!!! Actually, I did not walk, as by this time, I was in a wheelchair.

This doctor had left the room and gone to do the very same thing that the ER doctor did. He called my family doctor who had lied to cover his tracks because he had been misdiagnosing me for an entire year!!! I had such a lawsuit against this man. This doctor has no idea how very lucky he is that I never pursued this. But I know that my God is a just God, and He took care of this doctor for me. For what he did was very bad, and I am a child of the King, and I know that my Father saw what this man did to His daughter!!!

When I left this office, I was done. I was through with five full years of battling for my life. I went home that day and I called my one cousin, who is also my spiritual sister in Christ, and I just said, "I am done."

She said, "No, you're not. You will go to my doctor!" So she then made me go to her orthopedic doctor. Now what is crazy is he ordered an MRI, and I expected it to say what it always said in that my spine had all these problems. Well, let me just tell you, our enemy never ever stops. I have this report to this day. This report said, "This woman is perfectly normal."

Wow!!! Really? Whose MRI are we reading here, guys? For it truly is not mine! It had my name on it though. Thank our Lord and Savior that He alone is in charge of my life!!! The doctor that my cousin had taken me to was a regular orthopedic doctor and could not read MRIs. All he could do was read the reports. I will never forget the words he said to me, "I do not believe this report. (Oh, thank you, Jesus.) I want you to call an orthopedic surgeon immediately and take him the actual MRI."

For the very first time in all these years, I actually had found a doctor that not only cared about what was going on but knew that I was not making anything up and what was going on was very real. I actually felt I may have a chance.

So I went home and called my dad's surgeon's office again, but told them not to give me that same associate again. They did not. This time, I got my dad's surgeon, who was the head surgeon. When he found out what happened in the prior visit, I can tell you this, the associate was not in the office on my next visit. Coincidence? I don't think so. My Heavenly Father? I think so! Anyway I went right away to this doctor, and when he actually saw my MRI, he scheduled immediate surgery.

By this time, I could barely walk as it had become so very bad. I was permanently in the wheelchair now. After surgery, he said to me, "You were one messed-up little girl with a lot of nerve damage." He had cut me wide open both front and back to place my first set of hardware. I had six long months of rehab and physical therapy to learn how to reuse my legs again. Then in the fall of that year, I had my second spinal surgery to have my first of two cervical surgeries.

One year later, I had my second cervical surgery. Now my neck is completely plated, with the exception of the level right next to the brain. When this lady goes for X-rays, the technicians always say, "Gee, you have some cool hardware."

"Yes, I do!"

So it took me over six years to get correctly diagnosed and to have my first surgery to get relief. During this time, I had been trying to get my social security disability, and they said because no one had correctly diagnosed me during this time that I cannot collect my disability because my insurance benefits from the SSA had expired after five years. So I add this to this story for anyone just in case you are ever in this position to know that, get it in before that five-year mark. I am fully qualified and should be able to collect, but your insurance for disability only goes for five years from your last day of employment. Go figure that one out. But I have a greater insurance policy, and it is called Jesus Christ. I will not worry about tomorrow. I only added that for any that are going through your battles with the SSA.

But my God is greater, and even though this time was a very hard one, and many battles that I endured to find answers and to bet to a place where I needed to be, as I look back now, I still know that even during this time I was still doing the work that the Lord would have me to do. No matter how hard I try to substantiate something, hindsight is 20/20, and I just have to say that all of it has been for God's purpose, and the "handwriting has been on the wall."

Ding-ding…Round 4! The enemy loses…God wins! ☺

7

Major Healing Miracle #2
Ding-Ding…Round 5

I had two surgeries, one in 1998 and 1999. By May
of 2000, we had gone on our twenty-fifth wedding
anniversary to Charlotte, North Carolina. I had
planned this for a long time, and we had both looked
forward to it. It was during our trip there that we were at the
Charlotte Motor Speedway and they actually had to take
me out of there by ambulance. Not only was I extremely
embarrassed, but I had no idea what was happening to me.
But this entire trip turned very bad. It was during this trip
that the pain began with my RSD. This is Reflex Sympathy
Dystrophy. I had never even heard of such a thing before,
but I had it, and I had it good. It comes from either injuries,
surgeries, or other various ways. It comes in stages, with
stage 4 being a terminal stage. It is very, very painful. I
cannot even begin to explain the pain that comes with this
one. I can remember times when the pain was so bad that I

could do nothing more than cover my face and scream into a pillow. The pain of RSD is nothing that I would want for anyone that I know to go through. You pray for the Lord to take you home.

On top of the RSD, I ended up with MS or Multiple Sclerosis. Fibromyalgia, Chronic Pain Syndrome, oh, you name it, they had a name for it. But the first two were the priorities and my majors. But on top of those, my spinal column was still deteriorating at an alarming rate. You see, I have had the Degenerative Disk Disease. Since I was twelve years old. Now everyone has this disease in their bodies, so everyone has degenerative disk disease.. But usually, it only happens as we age. This is why older people lose stature. That is why I think it is funny if I hear someone say that if they are in their fifties or sixties. I just want to say, "Ya think!" Now I am not making light of those who have had real injuries. But others who have just had doctors tell them that because they are getting older and it is something to tell them. The doctor needs an awakening. Everyone has degenerative disk disease. Ask any *good* Orthopedic Spinal Surgeon!

Just to give you an idea of the difference. When I was in my early thirties, I had full MRIs and bone scans done of my spinal column. My spinal column they said was the spinal column of a ninety-year-old. That is degenerative disk disease. But that is because my injury happened at such a young age, my deterioration began to escalate at an early age. It also goes on to show us how mighty the miracles that take place next were.

From May 2000 to June 2001, we struggled to get a handle on the MS and the RSD. It became a losing battle. For someone that did not like to go to doctors and to take any kind of drugs, I was now taking many drugs to keep the pain at a low ebb and to just be at a low tolerance of pain.

When you are dealing with pain, they always ask you, "All right, on a scale of 1 to10, where is your pain?"

Well...I used to make up my own scale, and I said, "...20!"

Then they asked, "All right, at its lowest, where is your pain?"

"10!"

So at a normal person's highest, that was about my lowest point! And I just want to say something here, I have a very high threshold for pain. If you do not believe me, just go ask my doctors!

I can only say that I did all of this through my Lord Jesus Christ, for I do not know how else I could have endured through any of this without the help and love and the arms of my Lord and Savior wrapped around me at all times.

By the fall of 2001, we had to move to a single-story home because I was once again in a wheelchair and bedridden. As a matter of fact, the Lord had given us a major blessing by having one of my clients all but give us a home in the Poconos that was on one floor. I had now become terminal with the RSD, and the MS had now reared its nasty head in my life. So we were on a heavy road, but we were also making the most of it. Bob was doing everything from working to provide the income to taking care of me, cooking meals, and taking care of the home. Once in a while, someone would come in to help. We did not have a church at that time as we had just moved to Pennsylvania and had not gotten into a new church before I went down.

It was during this time of the RSD and MS that I was going through many, many spinal injections and what they call epidural steroid injections. I was getting them about every six to eight weeks. The only problem was I had left one doctor because he wanted to do these, and then I went to another. He said he was going to do "facet injections." I did not want the steroid injections, and this new doctor knew it. He proceeded to do them *without* my permission. I never found out until many, many years later. I found it out one day many years later while reading some old reports. But I did not want these injections, as I knew what was in the medical journals about not only the risks but the side effects of epidural steroid injections! I wanted no part of them. So this doctor put another name to them and proceeded to do them anyway. This man again is another man I know that my Father is going to be dealing with, for He has a large part in what happens later.

During this time, the Lord provided all that we needed for help. I cannot stress enough what I said in the beginning of this story about Bob…that the Lord has sent me an angel. This man has been through so much of his own personal trials on this earth, and he has not only endured, but he has shown the unconditional love of the Lord through it all!!! I know that this man has some special crowns and rewards waiting for him in Paradise…Bob was working, taking care of the home, and trying to remodel the home so we could move to North Carolina; he was doing all of things that needed to be done by both of us in the course of a day. But when things got tough, the Lord would send help. I had one close girlfriend that did not flee due to my health and another friend that came to help. Otherwise, let me just say that when you get sick, it is like everyone thinks you have a contagious disease, and they stop coming around. Both times that I became so ill and could not do for myself or get out of bed, it was as if I had become a leper. It is amazing what happens when you get terribly ill. I feel sorry for much of the Lord's church, at least for the parts that I have seen. I believe that they are going to have much to answer for as far as going through the fire when it comes to those who were ill and did you tend to them? What were your works like? Where is the church for the sick? If it was not for Divine. intervention, Bob would have been in some heavy-duty trouble.

But what I did have was a group on the Internet that I went out to create for RSD victims. It was called RSD Lighthouses. We all loved the Lord. It was my church, because all of my so-called church friends had deserted me. I was very grateful to have them all. I remember having them all by my side the night I almost got to go home to the Lord. It was March 18, 2003, and I knew I was getting ready to go home. I asked for prayer from my group. I think they prayed too hard. For as I felt myself going toward the heavens, and I smelled this glorious smell, but then all of a sudden, I suddenly felt myself back in my own bedroom and my own bed. Oh, I can tell you, I was not a happy camper. I wanted to keep going toward that smell! But the Lord sent me back!!!

It had only been a few days prior to this when the RSD doctor who was giving me the unauthorized injections was sending me to the RSD clinic in Philadelphia for the last stage, because he said that he could no longer do anymore for me. I had told Bob I was not going. I had told Bob that instead, I wanted him to place me and my wheelchair on a plane and send me to Florida that weekend for a Christian Crusade on the beach in Fort Lauderdale. We knew it would not be easy as I was in my wheelchair…but his sister Mary in Fort Lauderdale would help and get me there!

Two days after I had the episode with the experience of near death and that oh so glorious smell, I got on a plane for Florida. His sister Mary got me off the plane in Florida and she took me to her church, which was one of the biggest churches I had ever been to. On Sunday morning, we went to Calvary Chapel, and the pastors there all laid hands on me and prayed for me. Believe me, this church had multiple pastors, so when God's Word says, "Where two or more are gathered," I am sure, Jesus was in the middle of that one! Then we went to the Luis Palau Crusade which they held on the Fort Lauderdale Beach. There were so many people on that beach for a Christian speaker and Christian concerts. It was all for the Lord. It was glorious! First time I ever saw Third Day, Toby Mac, Mary Mary, oh, and just so many more that day. I called this my final pilgrimage. God bless Mary, Bob's sister, she got me over there and through thousands of people to get me to where I needed to be at the handicapped platform on the beach that day. But once there, all went well. What a glorious day that was. I was so thankful that I had made the decision that I made and went to Florida and not Philadelphia. Now I was ready to go see my Jesus, whom I had not seen in so very long.

When I came home, it was the same as usual. By June, I had another episode when I thought I was finally getting to go home to my Jesus. Once again, I still did not get to go home. Now I am getting upset. Does the Lord not want me? The normal pat answer is that "It is just not your time." But when you have been down the road I have been, you need to be walking in my shoes to be wanting an answer from the Lord as to "Lord, how come I can't make it all the way home?"

So now I am getting angry with the medical side of things. It was like, if I cannot go home to my Jesus, then it has got to be all of this junk stopping me. I stopped taking almost all of my medicines except what I absolutely had to continue to take for the pain and what I needed to get by, which was very little. I also stopped going to the doctors. I never had any adverse reactions or withdrawals to any of the medicines. I just stopped taking them all!!! I am telling you…I was angry and upset that I could not get home! It was like constantly missing the same bus!!! I still believed in my pilgrimage to Florida too. But what happened next was mind blowing.

When I took this stand, by July, I was getting up from the bed and from being bedridden. Then I proceeded to go from the wheelchair to the walker…and then finally from the walker to the cane, and then I was finally able to walk by myself freely by the end of July. By September of that year (2003), I was canning tomatoes!!! By the spring of the next year, I was helping Bob put siding on our home in the Poconos so we could sell it to move to North Carolina. I was even building basement doors and helping him to remodel our home. But truth be known, he did almost all of it. I did a lot of the siding though. He did the building. (But I did build that door by myself. J)

Ding-ding…end round 5…Satan, you lose!!!.

Intermission

Now I know we have the enemy mad!!! The Lord said, "She is mine!" What I still did not understand is why He kept healing me, healing my life, and keeping me here on earth. Oh, I was so willing to go home. I was so ready to go be with my Jesus. Finish our conversation of so long ago. I want to go home. When they sing that song, "I Have Never Been This Homesick Before," I could actually be ill. This is my song. I am so ready to go home, it is not even funny. This world is truly not my home. Oh, my friends, if you have read this far, wait…the best that the Lord has is still yet to come. Wow, you will not even believe what comes next in my life. Sometimes, I begin to wonder, am I living a really wild book, or is this truly my life? Then the Lord needs to remind me it is the power of my testimony that shall glorify Him, and it is all about glorifying Him!!!

But let me just say here that I know now what my purpose is…what my goal is…where I am going…and what I am doing…where at this point in my story, I still had no idea of the "why" and I still thought that it was the Lord that was "punishing" me with my spinal problems to keep me down because I was still dealing with many issues with my spine.

I was healed with the RSD as far as the stage 4 and the terminal stage and the MS, and I was up and running once again. I refuse to accept any of the junk that was coming across the doctors' reports. But yet, I still needed all of the pain medication to get through my days because my spinal column was still in bad shape, and according to them, it was still the shape of a ninety-year-old person. I was in acceptance of this, yet going on in Jesus's name. I wish I knew back then what I know now…phew. But that was not the will of our Lord and Savior. I will only live by the will of God.

My Word Never Comes Back Void

Oh, I just love this one!!! Two
testimonies that are not mine!!!
But they need to be here. ☺

We finally had the house ready and sold it in record time. Even the realtor's head was spinning. Now we are going to move to North Carolina. Let me just say here, that for many years, we were supposed to move to Charlotte, North Carolina. All of my bins were even marked "Charlotte, North Carolina." Bob is an avid NASCAR fan, and we always seemed to be in Charlotte, but we wanted to settle there mostly because it was warmer there for my health, so that is where we wanted to settle when all of our children finally were old enough and out of the home...Wrong... God had other plans. God said Shallotte! Must have been my hearing. J One time, we just went to Shallotte on a vacation trip to visit my sister, and both Bob and I knew in our spirits that was where the Lord wanted us to go. Now this was even before Bob was a Spirit-filled Christian. Believe me, Bob will be the first one to tell you that there is a difference. Now remember, Bob has always been a wonderful Christian man. He has always had a heart after God. I believe that he has always belonged to the Lord. But there was definitely something missing. I used to ask him all the time, "You sure you're saved?" Only because he used to be so afraid of the Holy Spirit and the things of God which pertained to the things of the Spirit. Just different things, I would ask him..."Are you sure you're saved?"

Bob would always turn to me and say, "Yes, I am saved. The pastor at the Baptist church took me into his office and told me about Jesus when I was twelve, so I am okay." Well, I did not quite think that he was okay. You know when you know in your knower? I think he just needed a good infusion of the Holy Spirit! Bob would never like to go to the Assembly of God churches with me. If he was going to church that day, we would have to go to the Baptist church so that there was no moving of the Holy Spirit, and we sat in the pews and sang our hymns and then listened humbly to the service and went home. I used to literally die when we would go to these churches, and as I said earlier, it is like going to a restaurant and coming away still hungry.

There is a song, and it goes…"At the cross, at the cross, where I first saw the Light…" This one should be Bob's theme song. J When the Lord moved us to Shallotte, North Carolina, we began attending a church that was doing a Christmas outdoor production of the birth, death, and resurrection of our Lord Jesus Christ that year. Well, it had to be the Lord because Bob, being as quiet and as shy as he is, got talked into playing one of the two soldiers at the foot of the cross. There is no way I would have ever thought Bob would do this, but he did! It was here, at the foot of the cross, that Bob found not only the full manifestation of the Holy Spirit, but the full meaning of what the blessing of salvation is!!!

Salvation is not just a word. It is a life, it is a living Word!!! It is something that you live and breathe if you truly love the Lord with all your heart, mind, and soul. Well, Bob walked away from the play that night a very changed man, and now he cannot get enough of the Holy Spirit and the things of the Holy Spirit. He has never waivered, never turned back, and desires more daily. This is how we should all be in our walk and our lives.

Just a quick funny story about the change that took place that night. Prior to this night in December of 2005, Bob and I always had what I will call "the battle of the radio stations.". When I got in the car by myself, the radio immediately got flipped to the Christian music stations. As soon as Bob got in the car, the radio had to get changed to his classic rock stations. This had gone on for almost thirty years. Well, this one night of the play, as I was on my way to pick up Bob to head for the play, he got in the car that night and I said, "Don't you dare touch my radio station tonight!" I wanted it left on KLove that night, and I just would not allow him to change it! Well, this was the night that Bob met the Lord Jesus Christ and was filled with the Holy Spirit at the foot of the Cross. From that night until this day, our radio stations in every car we drive has never left KLove since that night. We do not listen to any other music other than the Lord's music, and we just cannot praise and worship Him enough in our daily walk!!!

———◆———

There was another soldier at the foot of that cross on that night. Both of these men at the foot of that cross said that when they looked up at the person who portrayed Jesus that night, said they did not see the person there, but they saw Jesus Himself. Now I hope that our second soldier does not mind, but I am going to add his story here also. This too was a mighty work of God and one that I praise God for all that He has done with this precious man.

While we still lived in the Poconos in the early '90s, I had been doing a Bible study in New Jersey. During the time of this Bible study, my sister's husband (at that time), Jim, began showing up at this Bible study. What made this an unusual occurrence was that he was not a believer. Matter of fact, quite the opposite. I do not know if I could quite count him as an atheist, but he was quite close—let's just call him an agnostic. The very first time he sat in our group, I remember sitting there, and a few of us backed up from things he was saying, and we were waiting for the Lord's lightning bolts! Well, what happened next was that he began showing up week after week, I believe, just to battle with me about God's Word. They actually began calling it the "Mary and Jim show." It was God versus Agnostic. For myself, though it was quite the season in my life, for I learned much due to this time. So what the enemy meant for disruption, the Lord turned to glory in every way.

Every week I went home, I would be praying so hard, saying, "Lord, what on earth am I to do? He is disrupting the entire Bible study, trying to dismantle the Word and God…" But every week, I kept getting the exact same answer from the Lord. And believe me, I heard the Lord *very* clearly on this one!

God kept saying the very *same thing* every week…"You keep going…My Word does not come back void!"

Well, I was ready for him, week after week after week. Every week, I would be in study all week with the lesson plan that I knew the Lord was having me to bring forth that week. I do not even think seminary students study this hard! For I knew that I was going into battle come the following week, and I knew I had to be ready. Anyone that knows me knows that I get quite zealous when you attack the Word of God, so I would go back quite zealously with all the ammunition that the Lord was providing me before I got to the study that week. Every week, no matter what the subject matter, the Holy Spirit always had me prepared for every single question, verse, and subject that arose that week. During this time, this Bible study was growing, I believe just because of the debates that were taking place... yet Jesus always won!!! It was quite spectacular for myself because I knew what was happening. The spiritual battle that was going on was tremendous for this man.

This went on for a few months...Anyway, I had to stop the Bible study because this was when I was beginning to go downhill with major spinal problems and could not keep driving the distance between New Jersey and Pennsylvania. But the Lord had His plans in place for Jim. I know after this that he later went on to help at his wife's church in New Jersey with their sports before they moved to North Carolina. So the Lord began to bring him in to Himself in many ways even before he came to North Carolina. It was not too long from this time though that my sister and her husband Jim moved to Shallotte, North Carolina...His testimony is also a very mighty one for what the Lord totally did in his life, and it is actually Jim that would have to fill in these pieces.

Then it was about a few years later (I forget exactly how many years), I got a phone call from my sister Debra.

She said, "Mary, guess what?"

I said, "What?"

She said, "Jim is going to be a pastor." ☺

So you see…for every time the Lord said, "…Keep going, My Word does not come back void!" That tells you that the Lord had a hand on this life, and that nothing and no one was going to hold this life down. Proverbs 16:9 tells us that "A man's heart plans his way, but the Lord directs his steps."

But it should show any of us that God is so mighty that when He makes a promise to us in His Word, He is going to stand by His Promise, no matter what!!! I have seen it over and over and over!!! Not only in my life, but in those whom I am connected to. This is why I stopped to give you the testimony of Bob and Jim. We cannot control the decisions that others make in their lives, but what we do want to do is to preach the Word of God and truth as it is written, because as God says, "My Word does not come back void!" All we do is to obey the Lord. We let the Lord take control from there!!! For He is mighty to save! Amen!!!

I wanted to tell you about Jim because Jim has played such a large part of our lives here since we have been in North Carolina. I believe it was Jim that the Lord moved us to North Carolina to be near to. We were part of a church with Jim as soon as we got to North Carolina. This was one of the most blessed times of my life and also of Bob's life. I know that Bob misses this part of his life very much. Pastor Jim was very dear to Bob, and I know he misses this part of our lives. But as with every part of life, we move on with our service to the Lord. One day, the Lord will bring it all full circle with all of our loved ones, and we shall all be rejoicing together in a much better place and a much better way. One last note about Pastor Jim: he came all the way to New Jersey when I began to fail in my health and go into my wheelchair. I will never forget that he did this for me, and I know that the Lord has special blessings in store for this man. Even if he does not have his rewards here, we know for sure he shall surely have them in glory. Amen!

It was after he came to North Carolina that the Lord got hold of him completely. Things change in all of our lives and the Lord does things for many reasons, but being His servant is the best road that anyone can walk. Pastor Jim walks this road daily. He has a new wife now, also named Debra, and one that I love as if she too were my very own sister, which she is in my family of the Lord. But if you ever run into him…ask him to tell you of his own testimony, for the testimony of the Lord never grows old!!!

End of Intermission

If you thought the first part of my life was loaded with miracles and Divine. intervention, then you have not seen anything yet. This next leg of my life's journey is going to be like reading science fiction. But I assure you that every word of it is totally true and real.

9

The Best Years of My Life
Ding…Ding…Round 6

I do not even know where to begin as I start this next leg of life's journey. We finally sold our home and moved to North Carolina in 2005. After years and years of planning and waiting, ups, downs, and thinking that it was never going to happen due to health problems, here we are moving to the beach instead of the mountains of North Carolina. You could feel it was spiritually rich here. It was a good principality. I believe that there are principalities that are just pure evil, and you can feel it in your very bones if you are truly walking with the Lord. This happened to be a good one, and your spirit knew it. I was very content.

We began going to Pastor Jim's church as soon as we got here. Of that, there would be no question. We knew why the Lord brought us here. The one thing we did not know though was all the lessons that were on the road ahead before we would get to a place where the Lord would have us to get to. Our very first lesson that we had to learn was *faith*.

I know…I can hear you now…But you already have faith. Yes, we do have faith. We have learned so much more about faith in these past ten years that it is tremendous. The very first lesson that the Lord had to show us is that He and He alone is the one that is going to take care of us.

> *Therefore do not worry, saying, "What shall we eat?" or "What shall we drink?" or "What shall we wear?: For after all these things the Gentiles seek. For your heavenly Father knows that you need all these things. But seek first the kingdom of God and His righteousness, and all these things shall be added to you. Therefore do not worry about tomorrow, for tomorrow will worry about its own things. Sufficient for the day is its own trouble. (Matthew 6:31–34)*

To be quite frank about things, when we moved south, Bob's income was over $70,000. When we came to the south, he was making under $30,000 for almost the same kind of work. Wow, that's a huge, huge cut in pay. One that I was not quite expecting. As each month went by though, and I learned more and more to lean on my Savior, I saw His precepts working in full motion. For the very first time in my life, I actually had to take notice of this. I realized that in the north we had enough money and I relied on our money and never had to trust the Lord for what was coming next as I now had to do. Oh yes, I had to have faith in multiple ways for other things, but now we are talking pure faith that you need to turn your all over to the King of kings and the Lord of lords and say…"Here Lord, I can't do it." You trust Him getting up in the morning, you trust Him going to bed at night, and everything in between, that He shall take care of it all!!!

Those first years were daily miracles of the Lord Jesus. I watched as it was His provisions, and His timings, and His directions, and His supply that sustained us as each month and years went by. The more we were obedient, the more He was blessing us and the Lord was overflowing in His graciousness. And of course, you know that Bob and I are tithers. I do not say this in any kind of a boastful way, but in a teaching way. We believed that it begins right here. You cannot have faith if you cannot trust God at His Word. Trusting in God means that you trust Him in everything. He says…"Test me on it." But we need to give back to God the very best which is the cream off the top…the first 10 percent, guys!!! This belongs to Him!!! This is our first fruits. Notice what the Lord says that if you try Him in this…He will…"pour out for you such blessing that there will not be room enough to receive it." (Can you imagine that in your life?)

> *"Bring all the tithes into the storehouse, That there may be food in My house, And try Me now in this," Says the Lord of hosts. "If I will not open for you*

the windows of heaven And pour out for you such blessing That there will not be room enough to receive it." (Malachi 3:10)

I cannot say that it was not an easy thing, because the automatic thing to do is to worry about where your next dollar will come from to pay your next bill. But it truly never got that drastic. It was always "just" there and "just" enough. Praise God, that is all I wanted and all I needed.

Just like the one time the youth in the neighborhood decided to pull pranks in the surrounding neighborhood. They went around and burned down gardens and mailboxes. Well, I had to go and get a mailbox the next day or the mailman would not deliver my mail. So I went to Home Depot and purchased the mailbox, post, and all that I needed to replace the mailbox. The total of my bill came to $49 that day. I just left the store praying to the Lord, saying, "Well, Lord, I do not know how I am going to pay for this mailbox, as there is nothing in the bank, but I had to get this mailbox up." Well, that day, Bob got the mailbox up, and then the mailman delivered the mail. In the mail that very day was a check from someone who owed me some money. It was a check for $50. The Lord is so very awesome!!!

I truly think this was the one that sealed my faith for trusting in the Lord for just every single thing, I do not care what it is! My "faith" for my health comes later. We have so many different levels of faith. We have faith in so many things. But what I have learned over all of these years is that we need to roll all of these "faiths" into just one pure faith into Jesus and that He can do every single thing that He has said in His Word, no Matter what. We seem to take bits and pieces for what we want and then throw the rest to the side or to theology. No, my friends, All of it belongs to the Lord Jesus Christ. Every jot and tittle is the Word of God, and none of it shall perish, whether it is a part that you like or believe or want to believe. As for myself, if God said it, I believe it, and that's all there is to it!!!

We had moved to North Carolina when our children had all grown up and moved away from home. When we arrived in North Carolina, we had one son, Jeffrey, living in New Jersey and a daughter, Jennifer, who later lived in Florida. But it did not take very long at all until both of our children that the Lord had blessed us with, followed us to North Carolina. They both had their own homes and now my life was complete. Jeffrey actually got married and he and his wife had my very first grandchild, Tyler James. When they say there is nothing like a grandchild, they are definitely not kidding. This child was my heart. For many long years, I had only one prayer request to my Father, and that was "Dear Lord, Please let me have the pleasure of a grandchild before you come in the Rapture."

Believe it or not, this was my prayer for many, many years. So needless to say, when Tyler came along, my heart was totally full, and with my family all there, I did not think life could get any better. These were my very favorite years of all. J I will have more to say on Tyler later as he plays greatly into my surrender. For now, my life is surely complete, right, Lord? Right…Watch what the enemy does! I am telling you, sometimes I feel like Job, and the enemy was up there going…Let me at her, God."

After the first year here, Pastor Jim and his new wife Debra, Bob, and myself, and another couple, named Aaron and Beverly, started a new church. For the next few years, this became one of the most active and blessed times of my entire life so far. This was about 2006 through 2009. From being on the church board to secretary to treasurer. Food Pantry Ministry, Women's Ministry, this was a super active and extremely blessed time. I would call this the best years of my life. But I was a truly blessed woman to be totally surrounded by those whom I loved and that truly loved me in Christ. We were truly a family in Christ. The love of Christ was a real love, and the fellowship that we shared was a real one as we served our Lord in every way that we could for the small church that we were. I sincerely miss those days.

A few things happened which I want to mention during this time. It was from this point in my life that many things began to happen. One night during the middle of the night. I woke up to the Lord saying to me, *"Tell them*: s*top adjusting God's Word to fit your life*. Start adjusting your life to fit God's Word."

I immediately jumped out of bed and ran for pen and paper. I then got up in the morning and put it into a sign format and framed it and took it to church the next morning. If I remember correctly, even the sermon was on those lines that day. God's message matched Pastor Jim's sermon that day.

It was during the time that we were going to His House Church that my spinal column began to give me problems once again. I had never stopped going to the doctors since my surgeries in New Jersey, and I had never been off the pain medicine. I had now been wearing a pain patch for ten years and pain medicine for thirteen. Even though I was one very grateful person for my healing in 2003, I still had a spine that had its issues of pain and what the doctors were calling a degenerative disk disease, and I still had bad discs. If my spinal column looked like a ninety-year-old at age of thirty, I would never want to know what it looked like at fifty years old! All I knew was that the pain was escalating once again, and I figured maybe I had better go and see the orthopedic doctor for a change. Well, I did. All he did was to take an X-ray. This man did not even need an MRI.

This was in January of 2009. I will never forget when he came in the room and said, "Can you come here for a minute please?" So I followed him out of the room into his office where he had my X-ray up on the screen. He pointed to the X-ray, looked at me, and said, "You should not be walking... You have a collapsed spinal column."

The doctor must have thought I was looney tunes! I actually became joyous. Most people would probably have become very distraught or sad, cried, or something! I became so joyous and wanted to dance right out of that office!!! I knew that the reason why I was up and walking was the Lord Jesus! I knew it was by His strength and His might that I was walking!!! This was in 2009!!!

You see the enemy was trying to take me down by stealing my very backbone. But the Lord Jesus said, "I am mightier!" As I have said earlier, hindsight is 20/20. I was not aware then that all of my health issues was the enemy. I truly believed what my pastors(when I was young) told me. Now I know that my infirmities were not from God at all!!!!!! I am a child of the King, and the enemy knew this! He has tried to lie, cheat, steal, and destroy that which the Lord Jesus has come to make His own!!!!!! But guess what? Now his game is up, and I have unveiled his plans so now I can expose all that he attempts to do from here on out. Amen!!!

I went to church that Sunday, and I had a testimony and a half to tell. The doctors and the X-rays all say that I should not be walking, as my spinal column is collapsed. But the Lord Jesus says, "Yes, you can!"

So I knew that even though my spinal column was now not only deteriorating to the point of rapid deterioration, it had now collapsed! But still, I was functioning as a normal person every day. Did I have pain? Yes, I sure did. It had been increasing for the past few years. But I was no stranger to pain. I have even made my own pain charts. Where the doctor's office goes 1 to 10, mine goes 1 to 20. I used to go in and tell those doctors that they had no idea what it was like to live in the kind of pain that was a daily level 10. So I created my own pain chart. If I can find it, I will add it to this book. All I can say is once again, "Thank you, Lord, for getting me through all of those years of mighty pain." Forty years of intense pain has given me a very high tolerance for pain, but yet the medicines were gradually increasing due to the increasing pain by this time.

Ding-ding...end of round six. You think Satan would learn, he loses!

10

Women on Fire for Christ Is Birthed
Oh Boy, Is the Enemy Mad Now!
Ding…Ding…Round 7

As a few months go by, and I was driving down the road doing a church errand. On a bright sunny day in early May 2009, I heard the Lord Jesus tell me loud and clear, and I will never forget it:

> *I want my women on fire for Christ. For many are going to say, "Lord, Lord, have we not prophesied in your name"…And I am going to say, "…Depart from me, I do not know you."*

It is amazing how you never forget the words spoken by the Living God! I remembered every word that He spoke, and I knew some of it came from His Word. At the time, I did not know exactly where it was, but I knew it was His Word. I sure do know where it is now! I could not wait to get home that day and find exactly where this particular scripture was coming from. When I heard the Lord say this, I knew that this was going to be my ministry. I already had a women's ministry in the church, and this ministry was gaining speed to where we were running out of room for people to sit. So what I did was I created a second ministry, and I called it Women on Fire for Christ, just as the Lord called it.

At first, we began this ministry as a prophetic ministry. We met to study prophecy since my other women's ministry was doing normal studies. We had this one focused on prophecy. The enemy was well aware of every step I was taking…let me tell you, because it was only a few short weeks after the start of this Bible study group start-up that my next bout with the enemy began…big time!!!

We did not want to leave this church, but it was the Lord that eventually had us move on to another church. This was not a happy day for myself or Bob. But when the Lord tells you to move, you move. We loved the church, and we loved Pastor Jim and Debra and the people, but we just do not follow man. We follow the Lord, and the Holy Spirit is our guide in all that we do. We shall forever be grateful for the very blessed years that were given to us when we first came to North Carolina, and the very precious time that we had with Pastor Jim and Debra. Maybe someday, he will bring us back together.

Now the bottom is about to fall out. We changed churches and began going to a large church in Shallotte.

The worship service to the Lord was phenomenal, and that was what brought us to this church. Bob and I both are what one would definitely call "…worshipers." We believe that the purpose of going to the House of the Lord is to worship Him, to praise Him. To love Him… If you want to have a social gathering, you can have that at your local McDonalds! When we were looking for a church, we looked for the worship and also the message had to be aligned purely with the Word of God. So we had found Highest Praise, which for myself was a full Holy Spirit–filled Pentecostal church. This was almost the kind of church I grew up with, even though this one was a nondenominational church. It was also the kind that Bob stayed out of when we lived up north. J It was actually Bob's very first exposure to this depth of a movement of the Holy Spirit this deep. The very first service we attended there… there was an altar call at the end of the service. I knew what was coming. I do not think Bob did. It was so powerful and so tremendous. People were getting slain in the spirit all over the place. There was a message in tongues from the congregation and the interpretation. The service that day was going longer and longer and longer…I kept looking at Bob out of the corner of my eye. All seemed all right. The service seemed to be going on into the afternoon this day, but finally, it was over. When we finally got outside to the car, my first question to Bob was…"Well, what did you think?"

And my wonderful husband of many words said, "It wasn't long enough."

Praise God!!! I knew we had found a home. Bob, who had been afraid of that kind of movement all of his life, was now so hungry for it; he said that a service that was so full of the move of the Holy Spirit was not long enough!"

Now sadly, I only remember a few more services like that very first service at Highest Praise. Then I got sick. I believe that move was purely for Bob. It is what brought Bob full force into the realm of the Lord's presence of the throne room and taught him to worship, and this is why we are both true worshipers. Bob and I love to worship the Lord. We love to praise Him, we love to worship Him, and the closer His throne is to us, the more we love it. We live for it. We love the Lord, and we live to share His love and His glory. There is nothing like losing yourself in His praise and worship. I challenge each and every one of you to seek His face in worship. There is nothing like it on this side of heaven…Amen.

We finally joined this church. My grandson was dedicated through this church. We were going here a little over a year, and now God had blessed us mightily with our own business. We now owned a pool and spa company, which I ran until Bob came out of his other regular job. Then we both ran it together. Then disaster began by the spring of 2010. Little by little, I started staying home more and more. The pain seemed to be increasing on me, and I really wasn't noticing that it was actually causing an inability to walk until it was too late. Remember, I was so accustomed to pain and all the problems associated with all of this that for me this was all normal. It was not until I could not function walking that I knew. "Uh-oh. There may be major issues."

Is it me, or has anyone noticed that when I am standing firm in the Lord, the enemy comes in, like gangbusters? But you see, I did not know things like I know them now…

Then one day, it began to feel as if I had about a trillion fire ants crawling on my feet and legs. I knew I was in trouble. So I finally went to the appropriate doctors and had MRIs and the tests that were needed.

These results were not good at all. This time, we had to travel five hours away to a special neurologist in upstate North Carolina. By this time, I could no longer walk unassisted and had to use a wheelchair to get around. Well, once again, I heard almost the same words that I heard once before, only this time they were said to both Bob and myself.

"Can you both come with me for a minute please?" … said the doctor.

This was too much déjà vu. I was here before. The doctor pointed to the MRI, which I have to this day to prove to anyone who does not believe this…and showed Bob and I that this time it was not my spinal column, but now it is my spinal cord that is collapsed. This was not only why I could not walk, but why the feeling of the trillion fire ants, as that was the crushed nerve endings. The nerves that were supposed to be running freely through my spinal cord were all pushed to one side, and they were all stuck together as if someone had taken glue and glued them all together. They called this Adhesive Arachnoiditis…My case was in a very bad situation and Adhesive Arachnoiditis is also terminal. I also still had the collapsed spinal column. This, on top of a degenerating spinal column that had been deteriorating for years and years. Thirty-eight to be exact. Many of my disks were either bulging or in very, very bad shape. I had a few herniated too. But I do not worry about those. I have hardware in my lower spine, I think it is L3-L5. Then my neck is entirely plated except the very top plate, next to the brain. I just have some lovely hardware. ☺

Anyway, this time, I was anything but joyous when this doctor was giving us the news. I say this because the pain that came with the Adhesive Arachnoiditis was almost as bad as the RSD. Actually, I think the RSD was there too if you ask me. I was totally in a wheelchair now and totally bedridden. It hurt so much to even move me out of my bed. Just to get up to go to the doctors was an ordeal.

I now had a nurse that came in on a daily basis, and she helped to give me a shower, wash my hair, and helped me to perform my daily tasks that anybody should be able to do for themselves on a normal basis. No one will understand what this is like unless you were to be placed in this kind of a position. It is a very humbling position to be in. I prayed frequently for the Lord to take me home. The pain was very severe. I lived on morphine, methadone, and many other medicines for pain. But even as bad as it all was, as I laid in my bed, day after day, I had a sign at the head of my bed, and I read it often.

"Because He lives, I can face tomorrow."

And when I wasn't singing that one, I was singing "Praise His Name," by Jeff and Sherri Easter! That song became my Theme Song! I love it so much, I want to honor them by adding it to my book. Here are the words to their song. Look how perfect their song became to my life. Let me tell you a short story about Jeff and Sheri Easter if I may…

Bob took me to a Gaither Homecoming Concert in my wheelchair. I had wanted them to know that it was their song that was helping me to get through every day with the Lord Jesus Christ. Well, Jeff and Sheri did not sing my song on stage that night, and of course, I was unhappy about it, but it is understandable as they have so many songs. I still met Jeff backstage and told him how much that song meant to me. He went and got Sheri off the bus, and they both sang the song for me backstage, just for me! Praise His name!!! Then I saw them again next spring in the next concert. When I saw them the next time, they were both amazed that I had been the same woman only months before had been wheelchair bound and so terribly ill…I thank them for their devotion to the Lord in song and worship that has helped people such as myself. Here are the words to their song that got me through along with my Jesus…

>
> Praise His Name
> by Jeff and Sheri Easter
>
> When you're up against a wall
> And your mountain seems so tall
> And you realize life's not always fair
> You can run away and hide
> Let the old man decide
> Or you can change your circumstances with a prayer
>
> When everything falls apart
> Praise his name
> When you have a broken heart
> Just raise your hands and say
> Lord, you're all I need
> You're everything to me
> And he'll take the pain away
> And when it seems you're all alone
> Praise his name
> When you feel you cant go on
> Just Raise your hands and say
> Greater is he that is within me
> You can praise the hurt away
> If you'll just praise his name

This song got me through many a hard day of pain. When my hands went up in praise, the pain levels went down. It is an amazing thing how that works. You know why? Because when you are praising the King...demons must flee...

So now I was bedridden, and it lasted for two entire years. During these two years, I called for the pastor of our church for communion. He did not come. During this two years, no one from my church whom we were now members of came once to visit. I felt like somehow I had fallen through the cracks and felt very lost and forgotten. Yet I knew that my Father had not forgotten me, and I knew that my Father loved me. I got to see church on either television or the computer. That was the extent of my Christian fellowship, I had no live fellowship from my own church during this two years. This was now the second time that I was bedridden and the fellowship of my brothers and sisters was nonexistent.

My longing if the Lord allows...is to create a benevolence ministry for those who need fellowship either at home or in nursing homes, wherever they are. If they cannot get to the Lord's House as they once did and are hungry for those who were once their fellow congregation, I want to take the congregation to them...If the Lord wills, I am going to do this yet!!!! Until you are in the position of not being able to get to your home church and to not be able to listen to your own pastor, no one can understand the loneliness and the devastation of feeling like you are from long ago and have been placed in one of the "leper colonies" and that this is your life and there is no more. I will make a change to this wherever the Lord directs me to change it! For this is a sad state of the Christian church today!

If you would like to be part of this ministry, you can always contact me or create one in your own neighborhood! I know of many people that are falling through the cracks just as I did!!! What has happened to our churches?

I want to take this opportunity here to say that when I met Bob thirty-five years ago, I said, "God sent me an angel." I did not realize it then, but I had been speaking prophetically then, and I can still hear myself saying it and even the spot I stood when I said it. This man, who is a very quiet man, is one who has endured not once, but twice he has dealt with not only the fact that I was bedridden and incapable of functioning as a normal human being, and he had to pick up on all the normal daily household functions, but he had to also deal with the emotional fact that the doctors were giving his wife a death sentence. This has been done to him not once, but twice. Twice, he has stood by me, he has cared for me, he has cooked my meals, cleaned the home, taken me wherever I needed to go, did all the shopping, and all at the same time has been making the money to keep us going. This last time, I do not think added to all of that, did he even miss a night's church service or Bible Study?

If I had to list the God-given gifts that Bob has, they would be gifts of patience, tremendous love, and wisdom. Bob is like that wise old owl that sits on that branch and never says anything except "Whoo-whoo." But don't be fooled. I believe that the Lord has this man's ear. For if you ask him a question, he has the wisdom of Solomon inside of him. He is one man I would follow into any battle. But I just want to give my eternal gratitude and my love to this man that the Lord has sent to me over forty years ago now, and I plan on spending a wonderful eternity beside him, along with the Lord Jesus Christ, and the rest of my children and grandchildren. Thank you, Lord, and thank you, my most beloved husband, with whom I could not have gotten through any of this both physically and emotionally. May God bless you with all that your heart desires and all that he has for you, both here and eternally.

Toward the end of this period, my husband had run into an old fellow coworker from an old job, and I was so very thankful. Why? …Because her husband was a pastor, and he finally brought me communion. So after almost two years, I finally got my communion. At the time, I did not know I could have had it any time I wanted, but now, I know much more than I did then. Once they started coming, they then began to come every week, and then it turned into a regular weekly Bible study in our home so that I could have fellowship and "church." I thank the Lord for this couple. Their names were also Pastor Jim and his wife Bea. There was now six of us that would gather on a weekly basis We tried for a long time to honor them by staying with their church, but we just have different needs when it comes to being fed, and I know that they became upset that we left, but we could not stay and not feed the Holy Spirit just to please man. But we will forever love them both. By the way, Jim was an awesome pastor and a dynamic speaker.

I think you can say Bob and I are Son worshipers. or Son seekers. We go where the Son is!!! Especially where the Holy Ghost is flowing like water... Is that why we are now at the Beach?

11

Major Healing Miracle #3
God Sends His Anointed
Ding…Ding…Round 8

I t was during the time after they were coming to the house that in October of 2012, there came a knock at the door. I just happened to be up and in my wheelchair that day because my grandson Tyler was at my home. He was now going on four years old. You see, I would try to get up in my wheelchair to try to help his dad Jeff watch him when he went to work. Yes, it hurt to be up, but Tyler was used to me in the chair by now, and he was very good. We would both sit in the living room and he would crawl up in my lap, and Grammy would give him rides around the house. He liked this part. Sometimes, Grammy even left him drive. This was my little man, and I thought at the time, one of the main reasons for me to want to stay here on this earth. When the knock came at the door, we were both surprised for no one ever came to visit me.

The man that stood there was from the church that Bob was still attending, Highest Praise. I just barely recognized him, as I had not been to church in almost two years. I found out later that his name was Lephus Pigott. This man is a mightily anointed disciple of the Lord. I believe that with all of my heart. I will never forget his first words to me as he stood on my doorstep until the trumpet call of the Lord sounds…

He said, "The Lord sent me to pray for you!"

I immediately got excited inside, as I knew in my spirit, I was getting healed that day for I knew that the Lord God Jehovah had sent this man to heal me! I never had a shred of doubt that I was getting healed!!! I just did not know the when of it. But I did know it was an absolute!!!

As we say…I knew in my knower!!!

As this man prayed for me that day, one thing I knew for sure was that the Lord sent him to pray for my healing. I know so many are saying how was I so positive? I can give you multiple reasons.

Number 1 reason was that to that day, not one person had come to my door from my own church in two years, and now here was someone saying…not that the church sent him, but that the "Lord sent him!" As soon as I heard him speak the word that the "Lord had sent him" …I believed in faith that the Lord sent him and that mountains were going to be moving! As he prayed his powerful prayer for me, he also prophesied over me by saying, "Now you too will take this same healing power to others and heal others in the name of Jesus." That one I placed on the back burner for a while, and it would be a while later before I would remember the words that were spoken over me when he laid hands over me so I could be healed by Jesus. But remember it, I will!!!

So after Lephus left that day, I was excited yet calm. I knew that once again the Lord God had intervened in my life with His mighty power, and I did not know for what purpose. One thing I did know though was that the Lord was saying…" Mary, you're not coming home yet." Now I can tell you positively and finally, I was definitely getting a definite complex! I have now endured more than forty years of some very intense pain and trials, and I want more than anything to go home to be with my Jesus, whom I met and spent time with some forty-five years ago. Call it homesick if you want to, but I wanted to go home! I was so tired of living in pain, and the only thing on this side of heaven that had any meaning for me was my family. They were the only thing that was keeping me here in any way. I was still in my wheelchair, and I could still not walk or get out, but yet I knew in my knower that I was now going to be healed! The Lord God had spoken!!! I just did not know His timing.

Now it was right at this very time that my own son Jeffrey was having marital problems. He wanted to get away, so he asked to go to my mom and dad's house in Florida. So

Jeff, Tyler, and I took a road trip to my mom and dad's house almost the day after this episode of the healing. I was still in the wheelchair and my pain was still pretty harsh. It remained pretty intense, especially after an eleven-hour ride in a car. But as the next few days wore on, things began to change. While I was at my mom's house, my niece Danielle, after hearing about the gentleman that came to pray for my healing, would say, "Come on, Aunt Mary, get up and walk." She kept trying to get me up and functioning while I was in Florida. When we came back home, within a week, I got up in the middle of the night to go into our bathroom. Usually, this had become a tedious ordeal, but this night, instead of going for my wheelchair, I grabbed my walker instead. I said…"I do not need my wheelchair!" Then it was only another few days after this that I got up and said, "I do not need the walker." Praise God!!! From then on, the rest is (as they say) history. I have been up and running.

The first few weeks had been slow, and I went slow, but I had just laid in bed for two years. After that, you would never know that I was down at all. I began to get back to all normal motor functions, and even the pain was at a very low level, which for me was unheard of. The one thing that I knew was that my spine was as it was before and that the Lord God Himself was holding me up. I knew that my spinal cord was still collapsed, and I knew that my spinal column was still collapsed. Not only did I know it in my spirit, but I knew it because my body was telling me these things. I knew by the pain that I was having. But pain or no pain, I knew that I could endure the pain if only the Lord would hold me up...and He surely was holding me up. I was totally content and satisfied with this.

This became my new theme song, and every time we sang it in praise and worship, I had all I could do not to fall out on the floor...

> I Will Climb This Mountain with My Hands Wide Open
>
> I lean not on my own understanding
> My life is in the hands of the Maker of heaven
>
> I give it all to You God
> trusting that you'll make something beautiful out of me
>
> There's nothing I hold on to
> There's nothing I hold on to
> There's nothing I hold on to
> There's nothing I hold on to
>
> I will climb this mountain with my hands wide open
> I will climb this mountain with my hands wide open
>
> —The Climb, Will Reagan and the United Pursuit

This is taking nothing away from my "Praise His Name," for that is still also my song, and also my "Because He Lives," but this song, when I heard it, was totally written for me. I am climbing this mountain with my hands wide open, and there is nothing I hold on to anymore except the Lord Jesus Christ Himself! For He Himself is holding me up every day that I walk, and every step that I take, and every day that I now go. For someone that had to hold on to something for every step that she took prior to October of 2012, unless you walked in my shoes, you will not understand how this song reaches down into the very soul of my being and grips my spirit and says that this one belongs to you, my girl…

So now I am not leaning on my understanding, but leaning on His understanding, and His Word, and every Word that He has written and every Word that He is giving to me almost on a daily basis now. For months on end, it was just a learning process, and it was like I had gone back to school and the Lord God Himself was my teacher. The Holy Spirit was my closest companion and teaching me daily. Even though I had been a Bible student now almost forty-five years, I still had many lessons to learn to apply to myself. Many teachings from doctrines from many churches down through the years that needed to be sorted out and to be brought back to just one doctrine: God's Word!

I anxiously await to see the next phase.

8…9…10…and you're out, Satan!!!
Bout and game over!!!!
End round 8!

12

Now It's New Life…New Battleground!

I felt like Lazarus after Jesus raised him from the dead. Absolutely no one can understand the feelings or the magnitude of the love and grace that I felt by our Lord Jesus Christ after this tremendous, miraculous healing that He had just bestowed on me once again. I was heading home, and for the second time in my life, I was with a terminal illness and given a death sentence. For the second time in my life, the Lord sent down His healing love and said…No, you have work to do…." I knew He said that the last time too, but I also still knew that my spinal problems were escalating at a rapid pace. The last healing healed the RSD and the MS, but the spinal column still remained deteriorating. Why…I had no idea. I always thought, just like Paul, that this was going to "be my thorn." You see, as I said earlier, I believed, just as pastors in my early years had taught that when we had illnesses, even chronic ones, we were like Paul, and we needed to endure, like Paul.

I could do a whole chapter right here about how Paul's thorn was not an illness!

> *Therefore, in order to keep me from becoming conceited, I was given a thorn in my flesh, a messenger of Satan, to torment me." (2 Corinthians 12:7)*

I shall touch slightly on this at the end of the book, but not here.

As the weeks went by and my legs were becoming stronger, I was elated at once again being freed from the chains of my bed and my bedroom. Those whom I ran into were simply astounded to see me up and walking again. Hence my super testimony begins for the Lord…we are going to get a little wild and crazy from here. I need to explain to everyone reading this book that if you think the miracles have been mighty and almost unbelievable, wait until you see what is coming.

I have walked with the Lord for forty years, and I have loved the Lord for forty years. Yes, I had some times when I had trials and problems through which He brought me through each and every one in the early years. Then when the enemy could no longer take me down by the world's means, he used my health. So for twenty-five years, it has been a severe battle between me and my body. I kept going though for the Lord through all of those twenty-five years, with the exception of the times when I could not walk. Even then, I had my computer and would be running

Internet-based Christian support groups (this was through the RSD). But I always loved the Lord and considered myself to be a good Christian person.

But, my friend, I can now tell you something, and I am not ashamed to tell you, I just wish I had known it so much sooner, as I have so many wasted years of my life. There is being a Christian, and loving the Lord, and there is being a Child of God, under surrender to the Living God, and there is nothing in your life that has first place except God Almighty Himself. Both are children of God. Both shall go to heaven if they are to die today, but both shall live very different lives. Oh, I know I can hear everyone saying, "But of course, God is first in my life!" ...Really? ...How much time do you spend with (loving, thinking about, doing for, etc.) God and how much time do you spend with (loving, thinking about, doing for, etc.) ...let's say, your children or your grandchildren? Your spouse? Your friends? Even your work? Your heart is where your time is. When you begin to spend your first fruits of time with the Lord Jesus and give Him your quality time, instead of whatever is left over, you just may find out that your life may begin to change. It was during this time that I not only wanted to spend my time with the Lord, but I also had so many things from the Lord, now I wanted to know. This time, I wanted to get some answers to my questions. This was the second time that He had risen me from a terminal bedridden condition, and I needed to know the "why" of it. My dear Lord Jesus was beginning to give me a complex. I just did not think that He wanted me with Him at all. I just could not figure out, if it was His will that I had the problem, then why couldn't I get out of the pain and go home. My relationship with the Lord began to change dramatically.

Remember at the beginning of my story, I actually had a meeting with Jesus, and to this day, I have no idea what we spoke about, but now, more so than ever, I cannot wait to see what it was that we spoke about that day, so very long ago! One thing I do know…I believe the enemy heard every word that was said!!! One thing I can say is that since this miraculous healing, things have changed drastically in my life, my spiritual life, and my entire realm of being. I had so many questions for my Lord after this healing, and the Lord has had many lessons for me. The very first lesson that the Lord spoke to me was that:

> *"I was not the one that was taking you down each time and trying to destroy you, it was the enemy all these years that was taking you down each time. You shall now finish the course set for you, and the enemy will not take you down again."*

Then the Holy Spirit took me and reaffirmed that it was Jesus who took the stripes on His back for our infirmities and that by His stripes, we are healed.

> *But He was wounded for our transgressions, He was bruised for our iniquities; The chastisement for*

> *our peace was upon Him, And by His stripes we are*
> *healed. (Isaiah 53:5)*

The Lord and Savior went to the cross for our salvation, and when He did, He suffered many lashes of an instrument that no human should ever endure. He did so that we are healed. Not that we "can be" healed or that we "may be" healed. He most definitely did not say so that we "might be" healed! God said in His word…"And by His stripes we are healed."

As a matter of fact, if you look up in Merriam Webster's Dictionary, the meaning of the word *are*, you will find one prominent word there…*be*. So for all the "can be's,"…"may be's" and…"might be's,"…there is no other word there except just the *be*!!! You shall *be* healed!!! Now isn't that just quite something!!! Our God is an awesome God!! He reigns on Heaven and earth!!!

Jesus did not say, "Maybe…possibly…I might." It is an absolute. You will not find anywhere in any of the gospels where Jesus passed by one single person that asked for healing, and Jesus did not heal them. Now, were there many who were not healed? I am sure there was. For multitudes came to him in many areas…some probably went away without getting to him, some who did not have the faith to go up to him…but the Bible never tells us. So neither can man! What God's Word does say, over and over again, is that "…and Jesus healed them all." Even when Jesus fed the 5,000. He healed them all first who had need of healing.

And there was more than 5,000 there as this was only the count of the men. Don't believe me? Read the story in Luke 9:10–17. Verse 11…"And healed those who had need of healing." Every single place where it speaks of someone coming for healing…they were healed!!! Do not tell me of the things in the Bible where those who were not healed. That would be the same as our world today. Those who do not believe. But Jesus healed them all, and he came to heal them all. It is not His fault if you do not get healed, it is Yours! The healing is already there. He placed it upon His back at Calvary! It is only the enemy that can steal it from you! It took me a very long time to learn this valuable lesson, but one I have learned directly from the throne, and I will never let go of it again!!! You can defeat it all!!! I will show you how later.

He was teaching me that He was my healer, and that He "never gave me any of my problems, that was my enemy." As I said, this was quite the revelation for me because I always believed that my physical problems were my thorn, and I always tried to endure what I had. Yes, I tried to get relief from the pain, but I endured what my lot was in life. I believed if Paul could endure…so could I.

Let me just interject real quickly here that I have always been able to hear the Lord. But now, it has been like having an open phone line to the Lord. Even that part of my walk with the Lord has changed, which I will explain in more depth later. That still small voice which I have treasured all of my life, when I would hear it, has turned into my constant companion. Oh yes, sometimes the Lord gets quiet, and let me tell you, I do not like those times…It is like being bedridden again and being forgotten by your friends. But then you will open up His Word, and He will speak to you through His Word. I love His voice more, but I will take my Lord, any way that I can hear His voice whether it is through His Word or personally. We just need to diligently seek Him. It is when He gets quiet anymore, that I am expecting an explosion soon. It is almost like I can feel him planning my next move.

One of my major lessons has been that our enemy is actually very dumb. He is a very strong and powerful adversary, please do not get me wrong. I will be speaking on spiritual warfare at the end of this book, and you will read more on this. But when it comes to our sovereign God, he still thinks he is smarter than our Lord and Savior and that he can outwit God. What the enemy does not comprehend yet is that the Lord God is going to use him to do His will. I can look back now at what has been my road that the enemy has brought me down low to the brink of death many times and has tried to take me out. But just like Job, the Lord would not allow him to destroy me either. The Lord has had a plan and a mission for me. I know that now. I did not know that all of my life. Even when I had my encounter with the Lord Jesus at such an early age of ten, I did not know what that meant for my life. I wish I had met a pastor or someone that had explained to me about what that had meant in my life. But I never did. Almost every pastor that I met, except the one that was there that night, had a very hard time believing that the episode even happened. But I am asking the Lord Jesus to gather these pastors in heaven and I want to be standing by His side when He confronts them all, and I can then say… "Ha.. Ha..Ha.," with a joyous laugh and smile, as **Jesus** Himself will tell them how very real the encounter was!!! This is one of my prayers, and I know my Lord hears it. See you all there. ☺

13

My Doctors

Those first months were so miraculous just by getting back out into the world. Just the testimony to the Lord was glorious. Believe me, I made sure that the glory went where it was due. I am not quite sure what my pain management doctor thought, other than the amazement on his face was priceless. I know I shook him up quite a bit, and I pray that maybe someday soon, it may lead him to the throne himself. But I believe that it shook him so much that on my next visits, I began seeing his assistant, Dr. Barbara, who was a wonderful Christian woman, because he stopped coming in. (I think I shook him up too much, but the Lord's Word does not come back void.) I enjoy my visits to Dr. Barbara though. She calls me their walking miracle. J You see, they know that there is no way I should be where I am. They have seen my X-rays and my MRIs and all of my tests. They were there through the very worst of the times when I could not move. My doctors are the ones I do enjoy going to because not only are they the medical experts, but I am blessed also that they are Christians and they know what has happened, and they cannot deny the truth about what they have seen and have been actual witnesses to. Dr Barbara said when she first met me, I looked like a ninety-year-old woman. I can tell her…I felt like one too!

My family doctor, who is also a medical missionary herself, is such a wonderful Christian in the Lord, and she would be my witness any day I asked her to be. This is my Dr. Marie Wheatly (I call her my Dr. Marie). If you are a Christian, you cannot find a better doctor to go to at any time. She has one of the most beautiful caring spirits for a medical practitioner that you will ever find. God bless this woman in everything that she does. I have been going to her almost since I came to North Carolina, and she has watched me for these past nine years and the crazy route that I took. Her face the day that I "walked" into her office for the first time was priceless! I shall treasure it and her until we are called home to glory with that glorious trumpet sound. Dr. Marie is not only my doctor, she is my friend, and she is my sister in Christ. I am a very lucky person to have God's medical personnel to be taking care of me. Coincidence? I don't think so. ☺

I will never forget the words that she spoke to me on my second visit to her though, after my healing in 2012…she said…"Do you know what your other doctor wrote on the top of your chart?"

I said…"No, what?"

She said, "The doctor wrote...'There is no known reason why this woman is walking!'"

I just chuckled and said..."Yes, there is! His name is the Lord Jesus Christ!"

Recently, I thought she was moving on me to another practice which I could not follow; boy, was I upset. I was like who am I ever going to get who is going to believe not only my forty-year history, which in itself is absolutely crazy, but just the last two years which is not only crazy, it is mind-blowing unbelievable! The next doctor will be placing me with the men with the white jackets. I hurried to see her, but our God is such an awesome God that I just cannot even begin to give Him enough praise and glory here!!! She said that the practice that she was going to, I could go there to that office and I would not be losing her! You have no idea what a relief it was to hear these words! I should have known that my God shall supply all of my needs! He would take care of me, and He knew that Dr. Marie is the only one who knows who I am in Him, my faith, and my resolve to persevere.

Thank you, Lord, for Dr. Marie and all of my doctors that you have placed in my path here in North Carolina. I love my doctors and the fact that they all belong to you. I know that you have given us doctors to help us also, but you alone are the master physician, and you alone are the master healer. There is none above you...

People's expressions as they saw someone two years ago who was in such intense pain that it showed in every line on my face, to someone that was up and walking and full of joy unspeakable was also just priceless, and I never let an opportunity go by without giving the testimony of how the Lord sent someone to my home to pray for my miracle. Many did not even recognize me after the two years. Two years prior, I also was much smaller than the woman who now was a lot heavier from lying dormant in a bed unable to move or exercise. I had gained almost one hundred pounds from being unable to move for two entire years. Most of that was sheer depression and Krispy Kremes! My poor husband Bob who was beside himself with what to do to make me comfortable and happy anymore knew that I liked them and would bring them home. So I ate them. I never ate sweets like I did in those two years. I think I knew I was going home, and nothing else mattered to me anymore. Since then, I have lost this weight once again. I just stopped eating the Krispy Kremes! (But they sure are on my wish list for the wedding banquet.)

One of the top lessons that the Lord has shown to me from all of this is…

> **The trials we endure are the testimonies that we are to put forth for His glory.**

So with that being the case, then we should always stand tall under all kinds of trials, for we should know that it is our strength to endure for our testimony for His glory. For He shall give us the strength to stand! He shall never allow us to fall.

> *Cast your burden on the Lord, And He shall sustain you; He shall never permit the righteous to be moved. (Psalm 55:22)*

So this was my time of just coming back to full life, and my healing the third major time with the awesome power of the Lord. This was all at the end of the year 2012 and into 2013. Now we are going to get super charged...

Buckle up, guys...

14

Comes the Surrender

It was a very happy time for me as I became healed, yet it was also a very disturbing and heartbreaking time for our family as we watched our youngest son Jeff go through the breakup of his first marriage. It was during this time that I was going back and forth to Florida now, as my son had now moved there with my four-year-old grandson. I had helped to raise Tyler from a baby with my son and his then wife Tammy. I do want to say one thing about Tammy here, and that is, she was the only one that came in almost daily to take care of things that I needed. Things began going bad for them in the summer of 2012. The Lord's timing is impeccable though. Once again, Satan's crew came in to wreck havoc, and he turned out to be the loser. In every single way. He set out to destroy a family and a marriage, which he did, but God raised a Grandma…and down the road has other plans in store. I don't think Satan wanted this Grandma raised either!!! Especially in the manner that she was raised!! Are things the way that I would have them to be if I had a choice, no…not quite, for I miss my grandson and my son, but I must march forward for the Lord.

By March of 2013, Jeffrey was moving to Florida and Tyler was soon to follow with him. This just about broke my heart. For over four years, this child had been here and a solid part of our lives. I had one prayer for very many years…and that was for the Lord to give us a grandchild before the Rapture. Tyler was our answer to that prayer. We got a chance to enjoy him before this great event for a few short years. Thank you, Lord. The rest of my grandchildren I will enjoy when I get there, as I know my daughter has had one or two that she has lost.

As Jeffrey retained full custody of Tyler, I decided to help Tammy to see Tyler as much as I could. So I would fly him back and forth as much as his school schedule would allow until they got their court documents situated. I did this until Tyler turned five years old in November of 2013 and he could then fly by himself. By then, he was a pro and loved it! He even gets to go up front with the pilots.

While Jeffrey was in Florida, he met a new girlfriend named Apryl, and they planned on getting married in the spring of 2014. She is a nice girl, and I just pray that she will be a good stepmother for Tyler as he shall be spending many days of the year with her and Jeff. I pray that Jeffrey will guide Tyler in the ways of the Lord, for this little boy is very special, and he loves Jesus. So I pray, "Lord, be Jeffrey's guide, and no matter which way he turns, I pray that you shall turn him toward the path which I know you have in store for him…"

While I was making these trips back and forth to Florida in the summer of 2013, there came a situation in our lives which many people would have said to Bob and I…"You are crazy for not taking."

But those many are not Bob and I…This situation actually has caused hard feelings within my family because they just can not fathom the reasons why we would not go their way. But that is all right, as I shall not explain any further my reasons other than to explain **how** "God said No! I am going to explain the very best I can, so here goes…

Two things happened this summer of 2013 which would set up the rest of my life for the Lord. During the trips to Florida, the subject was brought up about my husband and myself bringing our business into Florida as a second branch of our business. We have a good business already established in North Carolina, and my family wanted me to expand a branch of it to Florida. The proposition which was presented would mean a huge increase in income for the company, maybe even to the seven-figure bracket. There was a major company going to come onboard because of my brother-in-law. The amounts were quite impressive. It would also mean that my son would be an integral part of the company and guaranteed a job, and I would not have to worry about him.

Well, before I left Florida that August, I had my very first vision.

In this vision, we were turning the corner in a four-way intersection. We had already made the turn but had stopped in the middle of the road and got out of the car. In the middle of the road, right in the center of the intersection was a huge dead snake, like an anaconda. We just stood there and looked at it and walked away back to our car.

When I got home, I told my husband Bob about everything that had happened. He agreed with me that we needed to pray hard for the Lord's answer on guidance, and as this was so very major, we decided to actually "fleece" the entire situation. We had not given them an answer in Florida yet. This went on for a few weeks as we waited for the answer to the fleece. Then almost at the same time, I think it was a Saturday when I sat down at Bob's computer to download a program. As I was waiting for the program to load, the Lord said, "Read Psalm 53."

So I picked up Bob's Bible, which was laying there, and opened it to Psalm 53. Bob was sitting in the living room, and I immediately went into him and showed him what the Lord had just given me as an answer to the fleece. I did not need anyone to tell me it was our answer in any specific words…I knew!

That day as I sat at the computer, I heard the Lord say, **"You're not going to Florida, you have a ministry waiting for you. Follow Me, serve Me only."**

I said, "All right, Lord, we shall follow you."

Then the next morning in church, the confirmation comes when the Lord tells me, just before praise and worship, I heard the Lord speak....*"The Devil tried to tempt me with all the riches in the world too...remember?"*

All I could do was to catch my breath and say, "Oh, that's right," just like a dummy!

This happened about the end of September. By October, my family was getting pretty upset with me. I do not think they will ever understand the decision that Bob and I made to follow the path of the Lord instead of going for the riches that were "promised" for making this move. But I know with every fiber of my being that we made the correct decision. Since this decision, our lives have changed so much for the better. Our joy is with our Jesus, and even though I miss my family, and I will love them right into eternity...I know that this is something that the Lord shall take care of in His way and His time.

Then comes my biggest and greatest what I am going to call turning point in 2013. My Total **S**urrender!!! It had to do with my beloved Tyler. My entire life, my entire being, my entire world not only change, it turned upside down, inside out, and into a world that I have never fathomed that could be mine in all of my wildest dreams living for the Lord.

It was a day in late summer of 2013 when I was driving down the road in my development. I thank God that I was in my development and not on the highway when this happened! I was having a conversation with the Lord. It was almost like the conversation that the Lord had with Peter. You know… "Peter, how much do you love me?" Anyway…

The Lord said to me, and I will never forget it: "**You do not have me first in your heart.**"

Well, me…I am going down the road, arguing with the Lord…I told you, my relationship with the Lord has changed drastically. I am talking to Him all the time anymore. We have conversations all the time. I even argue with Him as I was doing this day. So you see, some of you who think I am obstinate…I am even obstinate with my Lord…He knows me, and He loves me anyway! Anyway, I was just adamant that I did have the Lord first in my heart. I "thought" that I had loved the Lord first and foremost all of these years with all of my heart because He has meant the world to me. My goodness, I physically sat at his feet!!!!! I was with Him! I knew Him! There is no way in this world that I could ever deny him because I have been with Him, seen Him, talked with Him. So how can the Lord ever tell me that He is not first in my heart? How? Because He is Lord and knows us better than we know ourselves… that's how!!!

His next words cut me like a knife!!!! I was driving down the road, and I slammed on the brakes in the middle of the road. Thank God, I was not on a highway! The tears were by this time streaming down my face, and I was sobbing like a baby.

He said, *"You love Tyler more than you love me!"*

As I sat there crying and trying to understand how that had happened, he was painting me a picture in scenes in my mind with all the airline trips and not only the money spent but the missed church services, then he was showing me so many other things that were tied to Tyler. As I said, Tyler was my heart. I asked the Lord to show me how to make Him part of my heart yet not have my heart break. The Lord has shown me how to do this. It is as my own children. I love them also unconditionally, just as the Lord God loves us, but now I can stand back and allow the Lord to lead their lives. I will only be in the backdrops of their lives when the Lord chooses to bring me to the front. But now I have a supersized front-row seat for the Lord God Almighty!!! As a matter of fact, His throne takes up so much room, it squeezes out everyone that they are all going to have to jump up on His lap.JPlease do not get me wrong...God has all of these guys up in His lap in my heart. But God takes up my whole heart now!

This moment in my life was so monumental that I had to tell you about it! It actually became my moment of surrender to the Lord. I did not know it at the time, but what happened was that I actually committed my entire life, my entire existence, and my entire being to the Lord. Every breath that I breathe belongs to Him now. It was from this day on that my life changed. From the time of my healing, small things had begun to happen, such as my very first vision, and the change with my conversations with the Lord. But now, it was as if the Lord literally opened the windows of Heaven... Now things were beginning to manifest in the realm of revelations, prophecy, healings, and just discernment that was keen beyond anything that I had experienced before.

It was also at this time that the Lord gave me my ministries.

This is what He told me: "I am sending you out as an evangelist. You will also have the gift and ministry of spiritual warfare."

I can be very honest here, because the Lord already knows what my feelings were, so this is no surprise to Him...But when I first heard that He was sending me out for spiritual warfare, I was not a happy camper. I know the ramifications of this and did not want to go there. But yet on the other hand, I also knew why the Lord was sending me. I am not afraid of the enemy!!!! By this time, I was also now mad at the enemy, which now made it twice as bad! The Lord had taught me that it had been Satan that had tried taking me down for forty-five years! This made me furious!!! Now he (Satan) and his cronies have a major adversary!

So after I knew that the Lord was sending me out in spiritual warfare, I began to get used to it. Then I actually began to get good at it. I am not saying this in a puffed-up manner, I am just saying this in a way that I just will not tolerate the wiles of the enemy. Especially around me. When you deal in the spiritual realm all the time, you begin to recognize things more readily than others do, and you can counteract things more quickly. It helps in many things. I am now totally surrendered to the Lord in all things, all ways, and in everything that I do. My life belongs to the Lord Jesus Christ forevermore. Not only can Satan not take me down anymore, but he cannot destroy anything anymore that God has put together because the weapons that I now have will shoot down all of His artillery. I will complete the plans that the Lord has for me.

> *For I know the thoughts that I think toward you, says the Lord, thoughts of peace and not of evil, to give you a future and a hope. Then you will call upon Me and go and pray to Me, and I will listen to you. And you will seek Me and find Me, when you search for Me with all your heart. (Jeremiah 29:11–13)*

> *"No weapon formed against you shall prosper, And every tongue which rises against you in judgment You shall condemn. This is the heritage of the servants of the Lord, And their righteousness is from Me," Says the Lord. (Isaiah 54:17)*

You see in September/October of 2013 when we made a conscious decision in our lives to devote and to surrender our entire lives and existence to the Lord Jesus Christ, not only did our lives change, but our very existence began to alter. The Lord began to change our business, our finances, our way of living, and anything that touched our lives. What was very hard to do was to explain this to our children and others. Bob and I already loved the Lord, and this is why our children did not understand it. We still sounded the same, looked the same, but we are not the same. At least, I know that I am not. My level of surrender to the Lord has intensified to a level where I have never been in my entire life. I did not even know that there was this much compassion in a human being when it comes to their commitment to the Lord or anyone for that matter! I felt like I was physically walking in the spiritual realm half the time! It was now that I kept saying, "It is as if the Lord has opened the windows of Heaven." So very many things began to happen. From the healings to revelations to prophetic utterances.

Let me share with you one revelation that the Lord gave to me through this time. As I was in the middle of worship to the Lord, I heard Him, clear as a bell, even above my own singing, say, "Pray for the sway."

I said…very stupidly, "…Huh?"

He repeated, "Pray for the sway."

As I am a worshiper in any church I attend, I am usually away from my seat. So I went back to my seat and I wrote this down immediately because I did not want to forget it.

As I went back to worship, I could not worship, I was too focused on the "Pray for the sway." I finally said, "…

Lord, what on earth is *sway*?" I did not mean to be so dumb, but I had no idea what it was. He was quiet for a minute or two. Finally, He came back to me and He said:

SWAY means:
S—Spiritual
W—Warfare
A—Around
Y—You

"OHHHHHH!" Now I am really going to sound dumb! It's one of those! Well again, I went back to my seat and I wrote that down. When we got done with worship, I knew that I was to go home and have it placed on cards. The only thing that I knew I was to put on the cards with it was Ephesians 6 and the Shield of Faith. Here is a picture of the finished card that I came up with that day and had printed. I have been passing them out.

This all began just before I met Prophet Kim last fall. It became stronger as the months went on. Each month, I grew stronger in the Lord. Each month, I knew the adversary liked me less and less. Now, when I get spiritual attacks, I just start jumping for joy!! I say...Well, if you are attacking me this badly, you surely must not like what I am doing in the kingdom of my Lord. And to top it off... you're gonna lose...The other thing I say is that if they are bothering me, then they are leaving someone else alone that cannot handle them!!! Sometimes, I like to lead them on a wild goose chase just for this reason. Keep them preoccupied for a while!!!

You see, I do not care what people think anymore of who I am, for I know who I am in the Lord now. Bob and I will not tolerate in any way shape or form things that are against God in our home or our lives. We have chosen to live our lives for the absolute glory of the Lord, and we have chosen to surrender everything that we have and everything that we are to the will of the Almighty God. Whatever He wills for us and our lives is what and where we shall be. I know positively I speak for me, and I believe I speak for Bob also. Ever since we made these decisions, we have had all the gifts of the Lord poured out in abundance into our lives. I for one will never change this. I plan until that trumpet blows, and the Lord calls His Bride home to Himself, I shall serve Him with a passion that only increase as my love increases more and more as the days go by. If this is even possible!!!!

> Now the tables are turned!!!!!!!!!!!! The guns are loaded and this woman's ready for battle!!!!!!!

I want to throw a disclaimer and a prayer out here before I get to this next part. I pray that I can do this justice, for here is where the truly Divine and extraordinarily wild ride begins. Not that it has not been so my entire life, but now it gets truly amazing, and plainly speaking, just flat-out mind-blowing. If I start taking rabbit trails, I pray that the Lord will help me to write this in order, for this truly is the part that will bring all of this into a mind-blowing current place in time...And all, all, all the glory belongs to the Lord God Almighty!!!!!!!!!

15

Here Comes Prophet Kim Taylor

The month was November of 2013. I was still taking quite bit of my medicines to try to hold a lot of the pain just from being up and mobile. Then about mid-August, I also found out that both of my knees were collapsing and needed replacing. I was in a knee brace, and I also had a foot brace on. But glory be to God, I was still up and walking, and I was still able to deal with the demons that came after me constantly to try to steal my miracle!!! But dealing with spiritual warfare as I was doing more and more on an ongoing basis now, I was getting rather good at it. You see one of the very first things after my healing that would always happen was that the demonic world would come in and try to steal my miracle. First, you need to understand my condition. Remember when I said about the thousands of fire ants crawling up the legs? Well, after I got healed, for about the first six months, this would happen almost weekly. I would be standing somewhere or going to walk somewhere, and it would start. After I found out from the Lord who caused it all, I did not hesitate, the very first time that it happened, to say, "Ohhhh noooo you don't!!! You're not stealing my miracle!! Now get out of my body, you spirit of infirmity, or whoever you are, in the name of Jesus because by His stripes I am healed, and I am His child, and you cannot touch me any more!"

Let me tell you, within thirty seconds, the pain was gone!!!!!!!!!! Every time without fail!!!!!!!! This went on weekly for about the first six months. Even though I still had my normal pain and my knees. All of this I could deal with. But these demonic beings were not taking me down again to a state where I was bedridden and useless to the Lord!! Oh, let me tell you, they tried! The Lord held me up Himself, and I knew it! I was so very grateful for that in itself, you have no idea. I was standing by the very grace of God. I still had a collapsed spinal cord, and I still had a collapsed spinal column. Now I have two collapsed kneecaps and need a double knee replacement. But glory hallelujah, I am up, walking, and still functioning.

So as time went on, the weeks turned to months when I would have to rebuke the demons for trying to steal my miracle. I had not felt anything now in months. Then one day as I stood in the bathroom getting ready for church, it started. By this time, I was just flat out annoyed!!! I did not have time to deal with them! I had an appointment with my Jesus. I'll never forget how funny that one was. As I was standing at the mirror and I began to feel that old familiar feeling, and it was getting intense. This had not happened in a long time now. I just stopped what I was doing and started saying right out loud because I knew they would hear me.

"You have got to be new demons, because if not, you would know that you are not stealing my miracle, and I am covered by the blood of Jesus, and unless you want some all over you, you had better flee now!!!" I was so mad for having to deal with them at that moment!

But let me tell you, they left in about five seconds!!! I laughed so hard. Then I had to stop what I was doing anyway because I had to go find Bob and tell him what just happened. Let me tell you, my friends, the demonic realm is very real. Once you learn this, and you learn how to take control over it, you will lead a much happier existence here on earth. Jesus said you can whoop them all!!! You have more power in your little pinky—oh, wait, I am getting ahead of myself...(but I guess you can tell I am not afraid of them...any of them!!!)

So you see, a battle has been in my life since the day my feet has touched the floor when the Lord sent Lephus to lay hands on me that day so that the Lord Jesus Christ could heal my body. For no matter who it is that prays for you, nor who it is that shall use the gift that the Lord has given them to lead you to healing, it is always the Lord Jesus Christ that is our healer, and it is only by the stripes that He took on His back on Calvary that we are healed.

None of us ever suffered one day in our lives for another person's healing. Did you ever suffer that awful cat-o'-nine-tails for someone's healing? I don't think so. Your body was never busted open to the point of bleeding so profusely that it almost became unrecognizable!!! But our Lord and Savior's was!! So it is only His healing power by which we are healed.

Some people have what is called the gift of healing. The Lord will tell them who to pray for because the Lord Himself wants to heal that person. But every believer has the power and the authority given to them by the Lord Jesus Christ Himself to pray for others to be healed. Jesus said so. So do not ever refuse to pray for someone to be healed because you think that you can not do this. We can all do this. Do not confuse the gifts with being a disciple.

Here is what Jesus is telling His Disciples as He prepares to go to Calvary:

> *Most assuredly, I say to you, he who believes in Me, the works that I do he will do also; and greater works than these he will do, because I go to My Father. And whatever you ask in My name, that I will do, that the Father may be glorified in the Son. If you ask anything in My name, I will do it. (John14)*

So you see, being a disciple of Jesus means that we will do whatever Jesus did, and we will do even greater things. If you have faith in Jesus, you can do all things!!!!!!! Now that's a whole book! Please, I am in no way saying that we are like Jesus or greater than Jesus, because I truly am nothing! But what I am is home of the Holy Spirit!!!! So with this being the truth, I can do all things through Christ who strengthens me!! Why? Easy, because He lives inside of me!!!!! Thank you Jesus!!

Now I want to make a distinction between the kind of healing prayers that go on above and the kind of healing prayers that are coming through a "gift" of healing. Those who have the gift of healing have been given a special gift and an anointing by the Lord to specifically pray for those who the Lord Himself says to pray for. It can be a single person, a group of people, or a church full of people.

I know because this particular gift was passed down to me, although at this particular time, I did not know it yet. I did know though that I could pray just the same as others, and I knew a disciple's power and authority in Jesus Christ. I am a full believer in all the gifts that the Lord has given to His church. I have experienced the tongues as I said in the very beginning of this book. I have seen the gift of healing many times, I have seen the gift of prophecy, I have seen the gift of revelation, and as far as I am concerned, there are a few others that are tremendous gifts, and I have witnessed them being manifested in full reality. Being slain in the Holy Spirit...wow, now that's a joy and a full manifestation of the Lord in you! I have been there too. I am telling you about all of the gifts of the spiritual realm because they are all going to come into play somewhere along the line here soon. Watch, you will even see me doubt the Lord on one of them…

So many of them I have had firsthand knowledge of, but until I ran into my experience with Prophet Kim Taylor, I was yet to have my full awakening into the complete realm of all the spiritual gifts that the Lord could manifest onto one person. Not only was I to witness these gifts, but I believe that He was also to have me to learn a few hardcore lessons from this amazing and truly anointed woman of the Lord God. I now thank the Lord, and I thank Prophet Kim for being the woman that she is in the Lord. She remains steadfast to her calling to the Lord Jesus Christ, no matter what the obstacles, no matter what the trials, and I pray that God will bless her always, and I pray that until that trumpet blows, her days shall be graced with a lighter load, and her helpers shall be many. Amen.

By now, we had been attending the Local Assembly of God church on Sunday nights for two months on a Sunday night because our church did not have Sunday night services. Many churches do not have Sunday night services in our area anymore, and I think this is so very sad. Well, on this one Sunday night in early November 2013, we walked into Beach Assembly of God in Ocean Isle Beach. Oh, my, my, my!!! First of all, let me tell you the very first problem that I had. I found out that we were having a woman prophet that night. Well, my spirit went right downhill. Sometimes, it is hard to erase years of church teaching. I did not know what to think. But this church was as excited as anything I had ever seen in a small church. You would have thought Billy Graham was there that night.

We began with worship, and as she began to speak, you just felt the anointing coming from her. I began to relax as I could feel the anointing. I knew there was nothing wrong with women prophets as I had been taught all my life. That was lesson number one!!!

God makes no distinction between male and female! He wants those who love Him. Does He want order and protocol in His house…He sure does. But that does not mean that when the Lord gives a woman a Word to give to others that she is to keep her mouth shut! That woman will be more accountable for keeping her mouth shut than for blaring it from the rooftops!!!! God makes us who we are…I for one am not arguing against the Lord. But I can sure tell you some males that will…During this whole episode, I have learned that nothing is stopping me now. Prophet Kim has been my guide, so to speak, to show me that when the Lord shows you that you have a job to do, you do not let man stop you. And I do not mean man as in "male." I am saying mankind. You just proceed on the road that you know God has placed you on, and the obstacles that come up, and believe me they will come up, God will take care of…for it is His road…

The next lesson God had for me was a little harder. Prophet Kim was getting a little…ummm, let's just call it "deep" in her service. She was in a great healing service, and everyone there who knew her was ecstatic. I did not know her, so I was totally reserving my opinion. Oh, Prophet Kim, if you ever read this, forgive me for what I say next. My husband Bob and I were sitting on the front row, and I was watching this very exuberant woman go all over the church prophesying, preaching, and just being a wonderfully anointed woman of God. People were getting slain in the Spirit from the anointing coming from this powerful woman. Then she came down the aisle that was right next to Bob and myself. The next fifteen minutes changed my life. But first, I had to learn some lessons.

As Prophet Kim stood about maybe five aisles back, she was standing there and she was talking about the Pool of Bethesda. I will never forget the words that she said that night.

Prophet Kim said, "There is an angel here stirring up the waters, and if there is anyone here that needs any body parts, get yourself over here right now and get yours!!!"

Oh, my word!!!! It was like a cattle stampede on a Texas ranch. Almost the entire church got up and ran over to that aisle. It was such a small aisle too! All I know is there was a bunch of people. Even the pastor. Well, let me tell you my reaction to all of this…. My exact words as I leaned over to Bob were "Bob, that woman is nuts, and nothing would make me go down that aisle!!!" (Please forgive me, Prophet Kim! ...I now know different!!!!)

Now mind you, here is myself, who has been through meeting Jesus personally, three major miracles, of which two of them were from terminally ill beds! Collapsed spinal cords and columns, collapsed knees...and I am saying Prophet Kim is nuts? I just could not believe that anyone could see into the spiritual world like that one. Oh boy, was I going to, later on down the road, not like learning this one!!! Phew.

Anyway, as I sat there next to Bob, thinking that our prophet who just five minutes earlier had been doing such a wonderful job, had now taken a detour, I was about ready to bolt out the nearest exit. Just as I thought that one... the next thing that happened was unbelievable to me, and I swear it with everything in me, I did not do this...but my body got *up* off that chair and walked down that aisle to what she was calling that Pool of Bethesda. I found myself standing right next to the pastor. I did not even know how I got through all the people. All I knew is I was somewhere I swore I was not going to go!

So as I stood there, and the pastor next to me, Prophet Kim, left the Pool of Bethesda and walked back to the front of the church, leaving the pastor and myself and others standing back by the pool. She then turned around and headed back toward the pool of Bethesda. If she prayed for anyone, they fell out on the floor. She came directly back to the pool and looked directly at me. She put her hands on both my shoulders and said just three little words that changed my entire life.

Prophet Kim said, "Take your recreation."

Three words that I will never forget!!!

As she said this, she sat me down in the nearest chair, as if she knew that I could not fall to the floor. It was an unbelievable moment for me. As I regained my composure, because first, I could not even fathom coming down the aisle. It had to be the Lord that brought me down that aisle!!!!! Secondly, He had a message for me! It was my final healing message! Third, it was the lessons that I needed to learn from a mighty woman of God that the gifts of God are true and mighty and the faith that we use for these are no different than our faith in Jesus Christ. For He is Lord over all, and there is nothing that He cannot accomplish according to His purpose!!!

So as I left the service that night for Prophet Kim, we found out that she was going to be there all week. Bob and I looked at each other and just about said it in unison, "We will be here all week!" When Bob and I got in the car that night, I turned to Bob and I said one thing. "Bob, I am getting a new spinal cord!"

Now remember at this time, I was still taking quite a few medicines for pain. I was still on my methadone, Percocet, and some others. I was wearing my knee brace and a foot brace. But praise God, I was up and walking!!!! Believe me, that's a big thing when you can't walk!!! People say how could I take so much medicine, but they do not realize, that is how great the pain was. I never once had the medicine affect my mind for functioning. If it did, I would not take it. My medicines went to all the pain, that's how much there was. That is why kids like prescription medicine for their drugs. If they have no pain, it goes to their heads. But when you do have all the pain, then you have no side effects. I never had any side effects, and I always had a clear mind.

The whole entire week was awesome. One thing I forgot to say. Prior to this week, no one at this church knew of my condition, or my miracle, or my story. Before this week, I had never told anyone there anything about myself. So there was no way they could have told Prophet Kim who I was or about my miracle a year prior. By Friday of that week, we had been filled to overflowing with the joy of the Holy Spirit. I am telling you, if you ever see Prophet Kim Taylor coming to a town near you…go to see her. Run… don't walk!!! Your life will also be changed forever. My story with her is just beginning…

By Friday, when we went to see her for the last service, by now, I was just as excited as the rest of the congregation. Now I, too, was full of anticipation for the Holy Spirit to fill the sanctuary. So now I knew it was not Billy Graham they were expecting…but the Lord. J It just does not get any better!!! So Prophet Kim begins her service, and as it had been all week, it was powerful. At the end of the service, she said to the entire congregation…"Now I would like everyone to come forward and line up at the altar so I can just go down the line and bless everyone before I leave."

Well, now this too was new for me, and I had never seen it done before. But by now, I did not hesitate for one second to a thing that she said. I also knew if I did not move, the Lord would physically take me Himself.

But Bob and I both rose, as we were still sitting on the front row, and we went forward to the left side of the altar. We stood almost at the very end.

Prophet Kim began at the other end of the altar than where we were. I watched her move from person to person, praying for each one in turn. Some of these prayers were so powerful that the one she was praying for were getting slain in the Holy Spirit and ending up on the floor. Now let me tell you how dumb Mary can be!!! As I stood there and watched Prophet Kim come down this long line of people, some falling on the floor being slain with the Holy Spirit, I stood at the altar of the Lord, arguing with the Holy Spirit!!! As I saw all of this, I was saying to the Lord, "Lord, you know that I cannot go down like that. You know that you alone are holding me up, and that I still have the collapsed spinal cord. (Like He did not know this…duhhh.) Lord, I would love to be slain in the Holy Spirit once again, but You know I cannot go down like they are!"

I kept saying it while she went across the entire line of people. You see, I knew I still had a bad spinal column and a collapsed spinal cord. It was only the good Lord that was holding me up every day, and I had the braces on my knee and leg. Well, finally, Prophet Kim stood right in front of me. Suddenly, she hesitated. I did not quite understand it because for the most part she had been moving quite quickly. But she sort of stopped, and she looked at me intently. Then she said, and boy I quote word for word, because I will never forget them!!!

She said, "You already had your miracle! Now take the rest of it!!!"

All of a sudden, her hand went to my forehead and Mary went to the floor!!!!!!! *Swoooshhhhhh*. And believe me, I did not feel one thing! Then in two seconds, she turned and laid her hands on Bob's forehead and he went down. Swoooshhhhhhhh!!!!!!!!!!! Bob never even saw what was coming, he did not have time to!!!!

So much for my argument with the Lord! I lost!!!! I should have known better after all of these years than to try to argue with the King of kings! He can make anything happen!!! But, my friends, as I was slain in the Holy Spirit that night, number 1, it was so glorious because I had not been there for a very long time due to my spinal column, and number 2, it brought to me a very strong message from the Lord...

As I got in the car that night, I relayed this message to Bob, as I just was bursting at the seams with it. I said to Bob, "See I told you that I was getting my new spinal cord!!!" I knew as I was slain in the Spirit that night that the prophetic message that Prophet Kim had given on Sunday night was the one that was coming.

This is what I knew in my Spirit as I was lying there with the Lord.

I was going to be recreated. I had a mission to fulfill. I needed to be whole and ready to proceed with the work that the Lord has for me to accomplish for Him. Nothing is going to stop the Lord's plans for me now…

So I did not yet know the when or the how or the specifics. I just trusted in what I knew just took place through the prophetic words of Prophet Kim because I know my Lord can do all things!! So that Friday night, as we were going home in the car, my braces on both my knee and my foot were removed, and they never ever went back on…Praise the Lord!!!! Also the very next day, the medicines that I was taking were cut in half. I cut them in half myself because I knew that I was no longer going to require all of that pain medicine to get through the day. I believe that it was the Holy Spirit telling me to not take them, if you ask me, and I obeyed!!

As I said, I still did not know specifics, as to the when, how, or just how the Lord would accomplish this amazing feat. But that was not a concern of mine. I just knew that He said it was coming. Now the next day was Saturday and not to get too personal, but as I was taking a shower late that afternoon, I heard the Lord say to me very clearly: "When you begin to run, it will be done."

Oh my goodness!!!!!! I could not get out of that shower fast enough! Matter of fact, it's a good thing we live on a dead end street! I wrapped a towel around myself and went rushing through the house, yelling, "Bob, Bob! Never believe what the Lord just said!!!!" When I found him, I think he thought I was stark raving mad! I was still dripping wet from the shower.

Now this was mid-November, and I had no idea what the Lord meant by this. I just thought that since at the present time, I walked very carefully, and I most definitely could not run and had not run for a very long time that possibly one day, I would just take off running or something. All I knew was that I trusted the Lord and this is what He said.

God says it…I believe it…That's it!!!!!

I just want to take the end of this part to truly thank Prophet Kim Taylor for being an obedient servant of the Most High God. I truly have never seen anything like her before seeing her at the Assembly of God in Ocean Isle Beach, North Carolina. All I can say is that I pray that I get a chance to see much more of her dynamic ministry before the Lord comes. Lord, help me to make my life half as worthy for you as she has made hers.

Now watch what happens to the rest…

16

The Miracle of Miracles!!!!!

As we go into the beginning of 2014, we were still attending the church that we were members of when I was bedridden. I was beginning to become slightly frustrated within this church as I just could not find enough to do to serve the Lord. I wanted to serve God with every fiber of my being. He had given so much to me and I needed to give back. It actually became a physical need for me, and as the weeks went by, it was becoming worse and worse with nothing yet to do.

In January, some women of the church were going to be doing a benefit for the American Cancer Society. As my dad had cancer, I wanted to help, and I figured that maybe I could help at the booth or something. Maybe they could find something for me to do. It was called Relay For Life. At the time I signed up, I did not know how large this event was, nor how national it was. So I signed up to help in the event. The event was for May 3, 2014.

By this time, we were now beginning to split our time between two churches, but we would begin spending much more of our time at the Assembly of God church as they had so much more for those who were hungry for God. This had now become our Sunday evening church and now Friday Bible study and other events. Within the walls of this church, one never had a doubt that you would come in and encounter the Holy Spirit, as God reigned supreme within the walls of this church. The pastor was on fire for the Lord, and you could tell that his heart was one that followed after the Lord Jesus Christ and Him only.

Even though both churches had an awesome worship service and both had pastors that could give some of the very best sermons I have ever been privileged to hear, we finally decided to make the Assembly of God our home for multiple reasons. The main one though was that I knew I could at least have the chance here to serve within the family of God as it should be within God's church family. My place is a servant, and I need to serve. The last thing I am is a pew sitter. Another reason was they had Sunday school. We just could not get enough of the Lord, regardless of how it was coming forth, either in praise and worship or in teaching. I was beginning to think Sunday school was something of the past along with many other things…But finally a church that had more of the teaching of the Lord Jesus Christ…

But just to add a quick note here, I know that I am not where the Lord would have me to be yet, but I am to be here for a season. We are going on in the manner to which the Lord would have us to go.

He has said to "Be still and know that I am God" (**Psalm 46:10).**

At this point, there are three things which are a certainty:

1. The Lord God Almighty is still holding me up every day!

2. That He has promised to make me a "recreation" and "complete my miracle."

3. When I begin to run, it would all be done!!!!

I spent every day excited, and if I had the chance to share it with someone, you can bet that I did!! Did people think that I was looney tunes? You bet!!!! They still do. As I have stated before, I even have pastors that cannot or will not believe the miracles and the things in which have happened in my life. Ohhhhhhh, but that will be my ultimate glory, when I get to stand right beside my Jesus, and having the King of kings confirm every one of them!!! Oh, I just cannot wait for that day!!! For me…that to me will be my paradise!!! I do not want any gifts, nor do I want gold…I just want my Jesus and Him standing next to me and telling all of these disbelieving people how very wrong they were. Then I can stand there and as Prophet Kim would say, "Hahaha…" J I hope she is next to me too; he does this sooooo well!!!

All that we are, and all that we have belong to the Lord, and we shall keep going until such a time as the Lord changes the route in which we are traveling.

———◆———

In early March 2014, I called my niece Danielle in Florida who worked for a doctor to see if he wanted to donate to Relay For Life. Remember Danielle? She is the one that kept prompting me that I could get up and walk after I was prayed for to be healed. Danielle is also the one was had given up everything to move in with my mom and dad so that she could take care of Him in his last days as he struggled with his cancer. I know the Lord has something special for this one. Anyway, as I am on the telephone with Danielle and I am explaining that I am helping out at Relay For Life coming up on May 3. This was her exact words to me…

She said, "Aunt Mary, are you going to run?"

The next pause could have lasted ten minutes for all I know…but in reality was probably only a matter of seconds! But in my head, I was hearing fireworks, and it was as loud as if it was the Fourth of July!!!!!!

Without hesitation, I turned around and replied to Danielle, "Yes, Danielle…I am running!!!!!"

I finished the call with Danielle, and I went to the middle of my living room, and there I proceeded to scream and pray and scream and pray and just glory in the Lord for the next thirty minutes at least!!!!

The neighbors must have thought the woman down the block has lost it finally!!!! I did though. I screamed so loud for a long, long time!!! I knew with every fiber of my being that on May 3, 2014, at Relay for Life, before it was completed, I would have myself a new spinal cord!!!

So as I knew that I would be running in this relay, and I was telling everyone what I now knew!!! Those who understood my condition said to me, "You had better start conditioning those legs, as you have not used those muscles in a very long time." Well, they were right. I immediately began to walk around our neighborhood as much as I could. It was not easy though. I still had my issues remember. Even though I was a lot stronger, I could not do the things I did in the past. Even going to work with Bob, I would only be able to sit at the poolside and write down chemicals for him and do the paperwork. That was all I could do. We still required a third person to go out and help him to do all the manual labor, such as cleaning pools and carrying chemicals.

We are now getting close, and every week, I am getting more and more excited!!! I know that the Lord has said, "When I begin to run, it will be done."

I have said it by now, so many times, it has almost been a daily mantra! I am trusting every word that has proceeded from the mouth of the Lord!!! And guess what? You got it!!! The enemy is back there in the background, and he knows that my faith this time is unshakable!!! Matter of fact, my faith has become so unshakable that now the enemy is going, "Now what on earth can we do to stop this woman?" And they are scratching their heads!!! It's actually funny when you picture that one! But it sure wasn't funny what they tried to do next…But I am becoming my enemies' biggest nightmare!

I found a picture on the Internet, and I have adopted it as my own because it clearly describes who I am…

It is a picture of a woman in a vest of armor and holding a sword. The caption on the picture says…"Be the kind of woman who, when your feet touch the floor in the morning, the Devil says, 'Oh no…she's up!"

Two things happened right before Relay For Life to try to stop the forward progression of the Lord…

As I was walking every day, and many days I would even try to jog, but that really did not work, I had to go on an appointment with one of our clients. As we were rounding the corner of a building, I went toppling down a sandy bank, which we have many of in North Carolina. Especially when you are at the beach, where I was. Oh my goodness! I was like, "Oh no, you do not!!" I got up, shook myself off, and kept going!!!!! That should have put me down big time. A year ago, it probably would have put me back in my wheelchair! If I did not know as much as I do now about spiritual warfare. You see I knew where this came from, and I went after it immediately!!! I refuse to let them get in the way of what I knew was up and coming!!!! You see they knew it too.

Wait…number 2 attack is amazing…but our God is even more amazing and outshines them all!!!

Never has "I can do all things through Christ who strengthens me" ever been more prominent in my life!

This one happened one week before Relay For Life (almost to the day)!!! You see, every spring, we always rent a Dumpster to do not only spring cleaning, but as a pool business, we always acquire much through the year that we need to dispose of. So once a year, we call one in to get rid of all that is around the home, and then our daughter does the same for her home. Well, it was the night before we were having the Dumpster removed, and we had gone to another city to see John Hagee. While we were out of town, our daughter brought in enough things to exceed what was allowed on the Dumpster for moving the next day.

We arrived home so late that night, I did not notice it. When I knew the truck was coming for pickup, I looked outside and just about had a heart attack. I knew they would not pick it up because I saw this large gas grill with two side trays attached, sticking way up over the top. Boy, I was upset. I called Jen, and they were at the store, and they said they would come as soon as they could to help. I also called Bob to alert him, and he also came home to help get this thing ready for pickup. But none came quick enough. I called them all before I made the dumb move (that's what others call it) that I made. But some say dumb move, but now in hindsight, I call it a glorious move because it shows the magnificence and the awesome power of our Almighty God, and there is nothing that the enemy can do to us (if we let him)! Nothing!!!

Anyway, as I waited for someone to get there, and I knew they were on their way to pick up this Dumpster, I said to myself…"Well, maybe I can climb up this six-foot Dumpster and try to pack it down myself!!!"

Wow, if I truly had to make a list of the dumb things I have done in my life, this would be up there on the top of them…but the Lord turned it around for His Glory!

The grill was on its back with both side arms lying out. Well, they were both connected by the gas lines. So Mary, with her bright ideas, began to jump up and down on the side trays with the gas lines. The harder I jumped, the higher I flew. The grill was at the back of the Dumpster. I did not think it was working, when all of a sudden, the one gas line snapped, and off flew the side table, and out of the Dumpster flew the side table and Mary, just like a rag doll. I bounced off the side of the Dumpster a few times and landed flat on the ground. I must have flew seven to eight feet in the air and landed with a super tremendously hard bang, after bouncing off the side of the Dumpster. Now, even though I know it was my own stupidity, I also believe with all my heart that I had a little help going over that side!!!

I do not know how long I laid there, but I knew I had two options…I used my now sore arms to reach around and I felt my back pocket…my cell phone was there. I could call my neighbor next door, whom I knew was home, or I could call 911. I knew that I needed an ambulance because I know my body, and at this moment in time, I can tell you this lady's spinal column felt like it was broken in pieces!! As a matter of fact, this lady felt like she was broken in pieces!! I said, "…Well, what now?"

Then all of a sudden, my train of thought changed. I started saying, "Oh no, you don't!!! We are only one week from Relay For Life, and the Lord promised me a new spinal cord, and I am not going to allow the enemy to steal anything from me now!!!"

Then it was as if someone started playing something like the theme from Rocky or something.. Now I am not talking literally, but that is what it was like. I very carefully got up from the ground as almost every bit of my body hurt. As I was rebuking and cursing the demonic forces that just threw me from that Dumpster, because I truly believe that they did! I began to walk slowly back into my home to try to regain my composure and my breath all the while praying to my Jesus.

As I was inside my house, I was just standing inside the door praying to the Lord to move the mountain that had just gotten in the way of His divine plans, and I prayed for the pain to subside that was at this moment racking my body. Believe me, I knew if I had called 911, I would have been fully justified in doing so! I was in bad shape. But it is the power of the tongue, and I refused to accept it!!! I was in the house about five to ten minutes just in prayer and talking to the Lord.

Then **He** said, **"Go walk it off.."**

So this is what I did for about the next twenty-five minutes. I went to the street in front of my home, and as I said before, I live on a dead end…I began at first very carefully, but then the more I went, the stronger I became. I went to the corner, turned around, and came back…the entire time I kept saying, "Lord, we're gonna move this mountain, we're gonna move this mountain…" I know it is the Lord who moves the mountain, but this was the way I was saying it. I just knew that this mountain was going to move, no if, ands, or buts!!! I did this repeatedly, over and over and over. I refused to stop until the pain was gone. Finally, the pain was completely gone, and as I began to feel much better, Jen and her husband Phillip came into the driveway, and then Bob got to the house.

Oh boy, when I told Bob what happened, I can tell you I have very rarely ever seen that man angry. Especially at me. But he was very angry at me for getting up in that

Dumpster! His exact words to me were: "How many times does the Lord have to heal you?" So Bob was grateful to the Lord for the healing that he knew the Lord had just given to me, but on the human side, he was very angry at me for making the stupid move to begin with. But as I said, even though yes, it began as a stupid move on my part, it ended up in another glorious testimony for the Lord. For I truly know that I laid there a broken woman that day.

I should have been in the hospital in traction if nothing else! But I said, "No way!!!" I had a promise from my Lord, and I knew that I was only a week away! There was nothing coming between myself and God's promise!!!

So now Bob has a new nickname for me...he calls me the Dumpster Diver.

<hr />

Now we are at Friday the day of the relay. I attended the Seniors Bible Study before I went to Relay For Life. What was really awesome about this was that it was as if the Lord Himself gave me a special blessing just for me that morning. For in the Seniors Bible Study, they usually do a song or two before they go into the study. This particular morning, for the very first time that I had heard them sing it, I heard them sing, "...Because He Lives." Now, why is this so important? Because it is the sign that hangs directly above my head in my bedroom. It hung there the entire time I was bedridden with my collapsed spinal cord, and it still hangs there to this day. "Because He lives, I can face tomorrow." This was the song that the Lord had Tom sing on this day of all days…coincidence? I don't think so!!!

It was just the icing on the cake!!! I knew that all was going through as promised by the word of the Lord. I knew in my knower! I could not have been any more excited as if I knew that the trumpet of the Lord was going to blow that day!!! So after Bible Study at 12 noon, I went to Relay For Life, and I began to help Ms. Kim set up our station. Ms. Kim ran all the children's activities, and Mary had opened her mouth for this event and let everyone know that she knew how to make funnel cakes. Well, I had prepared enough funnel cake mix for what I thought would be an army. What I did not know, nor was I prepared for was the response of the "army"!

I thank the Lord that there were two other women who were ready to step up to the plate and help me to prepare funnel cakes. After setting up from 12 noon to 6:00 p.m., we began making funnel cakes from 6:00 p.m. until 12:00 a.m. Six hours solid, I was on my feet making funnel cakes. Not only that, but somewhere in the middle of that, I actually stopped and took a lap around the track for my dad and his cancer.

We stopped making them at midnight. I could have gone and bought more ingredients, but they said "noooo" and to shut them down and now to enjoy the relay for the rest of the night. So this is what I did. I took many laps during the night. Some I walked, some I jogged, but most I just walked, as I was getting very tired, and for no other reason. Somewhere in the middle of the night, the enemy tried one last time…I took a nasty fall over a tent cord. We had a small pup tent in the back for changing clothes. As it was the middle of the night, you just did not see the black cords. They need to use white cords when doing that. I took a super nasty fall and injured my right knee very badly, but I kept going the rest of the night. I was even sprinting around the track by the end of the night. When you begin to run, it will be done…" I was not running all the way around the track, but let me tell you, I was one very exhausted woman! But was I running…I sure was!!! By the end of this night, I was running, and I was running for the Lord!!! I knew everyone there was running for cancer…but every lap that I took had a double meaning!!! I ran for the purpose of cancer, but I also ran for the Lord. My laps were for Jesus and the glory of God!!! For if it had not been for the Lord, my body would never have been on that track that night, so it was all for the glory of God!!!

In the morning, I helped to clean up the site, and I also went out to help clean up the track. I think I finally got home around 9:30 a.m. or so. I slept for about five hours. Then Bob came home and then I went out with him to a business appointment that we had that following afternoon. We had a spa cover to deliver and I helped Bob to deliver and carry it. This is not something I could easily do before either. When we were finally finished with that delivery and we finally got home again for the day, I was going through the house when I heard the Lord say very clearly: **"Do you realize that you have not taken any of your meds since Thursday?"**

I stopped dead in my tracks. Then once again, I was running for Bob…Poor Bob!!! He must never know half the time if I am excited or if something is wrong. J So I told Bob what the Lord had just said. I began thinking back when I had last taken anything for pain and realized that yes indeed, it had been Thursday. Then I realized all that I had gone through not only Thursday, all day Friday, six hours solid of funnel cakes, and no sleep Friday night, and constant going, then a few hours rest Saturday morning, then back up and going again. This was just unheard of in my life.

It was at this moment in time that I stopped all of my pain medicine. I only continue to take two of my medicines. One is due to migraines, that is a mountain we are moving next…and the other is for thyroid, which my doctor now says is normal, because I also believe this too was made normal at the relay, but I have promised my doctor that I shall continue to take my thyroid medicine to keep it normal. I told her, as long as it does not hurt me, then I will take it to make her happy. The only other one I have is for pain if needed, and I never take it. My doctors know me well, I will not take a pill if I do not need it! Matter of fact, I have turned back in unfilled narcotic scripts because I did not use them! I know many people who would never do this one...even Christians!

So anyway, as soon as I heard the Lord tell me about the medicines, and I knew what I had just been through physically, and I knew that I had been running laps through the night Friday night, I knew in my knower that I had a new spinal cord!!!! The Lord had kept His promise, and I was a new creation, just as Prophet Kim had prophesied six months earlier.

Now, this event left me with one issue: ...you see, the enemy is on a rampage!!!!! Oh, but I am on to his game now. Watch this one!!

Remember when I fell over the cord during the night? Well, number 1, I could not wait to get to Dr. Marie to tell her what had happened. I do not remember if it was Monday or Tuesday, but I know it was not long, and I got an appointment to go see her. I told her that I stopped taking all medicines, and everything that had happened. This was when she tested the thyroid also, and it came back perfectly normal, but I promised her to stay on the medicine. But by the time I did get to her, I mentioned to her that my knee was getting worse and worse and harder and harder to walk on. When she grabbed my knee, it did not feel so good. As a matter of fact, it hurt quite a bit. I did not like this one. Her words made it worse.

She said (and I quote), "Ummm Mary, it feels a little crunchy in there? I think you may have busted up your kneecap. I want you to go get X-rays of it now."

So I walked down the hall to get X-rays on my knee. The whole time I was going down the hall, I was going, "…I don't think so!!!" You're not doing this to me!" I was rebuking any and all demonic forces that may be trying now to take me down in another way. They just do not give up!!! Remember about a year ago, my knees were bone on bone, and they wanted to do two knee replacements. The one that was now in trouble was the one that had the brace on it.

So I had the X-rays completed, and then I went home. A few days later, I got an e-mail from Dr. Marie telling me that my X-rays were perfectly normal. Imagine that. J To this day, I am still walking on these knees, and I refuse to allow the enemy to steal the miracles that the Lord Almighty has given to me for both my knees!!!! Believe me, they try to come in and attack at the knees, and when they even begin to hurt in the slightest, I immediately go at them to bind them, and it stops!!!!! We must know our power and authority over the enemy, so that we can at all times be able to live a victorious life!! I would not want to live any other way again!!!

17

The New Life!!!!!

My life has changed 180 degrees. Now I am back working with Bob full-time. Last summer, after Relay For Life, not only did I go out and begin to work with Bob, I actually began to do my own route once more. I have not done this in many years. It has all been my confirmation to the divine work of the Lord on May 3, 2014. Last summer, I was actually pulling sixty-hour work weeks and still going to church three times or more a week. There is no way I could have done one day of this let alone six to seven days of this without having a new spinal cord and having the Lord making me "a new recreation." ☺

Now I am at a point in my life to where I know that the Lord has a road for me, and I am waiting for Him to open that door in which He wants me to go through. I look forward to the next Spirit-filled adventure in which the Lord shall place my feet. One thing I have learned, and one thing the Lord has shown me to the exclusion of all else… there is no stopping the will of the Almighty God!!!!!!!

Since all of these things happened, many new events have happened in my life. I gave my first appearance as an evangelist. What was funny was that it was under a tent. Not that being under a tent is funny, please do not misunderstand. Personally, I believe them to be about the best. I grew up with tent meetings and tent revivals with Oral Roberts and others that I cannot even recall as I was very young. But the entire time that I was bedridden, that was what I kept hearing the Lord tell me, "This area needs a tent revival." I cannot even begin to tell you the amount of times I heard that. Then the very first evangelist event that I did was under a tent. For me, that was a special event. I have mentioned this tent revival to multiple pastors to no avail. I know what the Lord said, and I just ask Him to show me what else He would like me to do and show me how to fulfill what He would have for this area.

It was shortly after this that the Lord showed me in a vision that I was not only going to be an evangelist, but I also had the gift of healing. We were on the way to church one Sunday morning, all of a sudden, I began to have what was like a vision. I could see me speaking before people. Then all of a sudden, I jumped down off what appeared to be this stage, and the people rushed forward. As they did, they were being healed by the Lord, then the vision stopped.

By this time, the tears were streaming down my face, and I am saying to the Lord, "Ahhhh Lord, I have nothing with me to fix my face!" Typical female!!! But the Lord knew my heart, and I knew what I was seeing. He was explaining it to me as I was seeing it. You see, I already knew that I could pray for people with the "power and authority" of a disciple, but now I knew that there was an even greater "gift," and this was the one that had been manifest back in January when the Lord told me to pray for Mark Thompson at our church and also a dear friend of ours. It was now that all of it comes flooding back. Remember what Lephus said about using what has been given to me and passing it down? Well, I did not understand any of this. Now it was as if the floodgates opened, and all of it made sense.

Back in January of 2014, before I stepped out officially into this new ministry that the Lord has called me to, I was still very much a novice in this new office. I knew nothing and had no guidance other than the Lord's. Since then the Lord had been an awesome teacher. So look out, world. But in January, I was speaking to Mark about something, when the Lord interrupted me and said…"I want you to pray for him right now!" You see, Mark had been very sick for more than a month with spinal issues and unable to work or basically move.

So being obedient to the Lord, I excused myself from the conversation and immediately prayed for Mark. It was my first time stepping out into the Office of Apostolic Ministry in this manner, and I absolutely knew that is what I was doing. The prayer was so powerful, and when I was done, I knew at that moment and with every fiber of my being that he was healed!!! I even told Mark at the end of it!!! I knew I could, because he was a very old friend of mine, and I knew his faith level. What I underestimated was the enemy!

The next day was Sunday, and I did not see Mark at church Sunday night. So Monday I went to his home, and I proceeded to spend about five hours with him, and what I call it is "kicking in his faith button!" Believe me, I know this man has as much faith as any of us and maybe more, but when you are the one that is suffering in the kind of torment and pain that he was suffering in, it is hard to believe that miracles belong to you. I knew that he did not grasp this miracle for himself. He was in this frame of mind…"Well if God wants to heal me…well, maybe he will?" I don't care who you are, when your brain is engaged with pain almost beyond endurance, it is hard to see light at the end of the tunnel. Mark was not getting any sleep due to pain, and his pain levels were just getting to be beyond what he could bear. Oh, believe me, been there, done that!!!

Mark made an off-the-wall statement to me…He said, "Oh, if I could just get a night's sleep!"

I turned to him, and I said, "Mark, you just named your own fleece!" This was Monday…

Mark's testimony is awesome in itself. But I will just say that I got a call the next afternoon telling me that he had gone to bed the night before and woke up the next morning!!! I said to him…"I told you that you were healed!" By Wednesday night of that week, he was giving his testimony at church, and he was back to work, serving God in the praise and worship team at church.

The healing gift has now been passed down to Mark. I call it the Pay It Forward Healing Gift. He now has his own healing testimonies and has totally changed his perspective on God's power in healing. You see, Jesus did not say, "Maybe I will heal you today," or He did not pass by anyone and say, "Sorry, I cannot heal you"…Jesus healed them all!!! And God's Word tells us that by the stripes placed upon His back…we are all healed. There is no exception to this. It is the enemy, and the enemy alone that takes us down. The enemy comes to lie, cheat, steal, and destroy. So when we stand back and allow him to do so then he will get away with it. I refuse to allow him to do so any longer!!! Even more than this is the fact that their days are numbered!!! This fact alone has given me more courage and fortitude to stand up against every single one of the enemy's minions that comes my way.

As the days and the weeks passed, the Lord was placing people in my path that He was sending to me for healing. As I was obedient in praying for them, when I knew that the Lord was telling me to do so…the Lord was healing them. It was beginning to be an amazing thing, and I still had not seen the vision yet of me getting off the stage. The only thing I was doing was listening to the Lord when He was saying…"Pray for this person, or pray for that person…" Then came the time when I did my first appearance officially in my evangelistic calling. When I did, all I had to do was to give my testimony, as that in itself is enough! The response was amazing. But it was not many weeks after this when I got the vision on a Sunday morning.

We now are fully in the OIB Assembly of God Church. The people of this church are what I believe God has described in His Word that He wants His family to be. Caring about each other, sharing, loving, and just out and out…there for each other when the other fellow is down. Are there problems sometimes? Sure there are, but what true family does not have a few wrinkles here and there. But when you are a close-knit family and bonded by true love in Christ, then those wrinkles get ironed out rather quickly, and the family unit stays intact. That's what it means to be a true family in Christ, and that is the love and fellowship that you feel when you walk through the doors at Beach Assembly of God in Ocean Isle Beach, North Carolina. But moving here, I have not told many people that I am an evangelist. I try not to broadcast this to many people. I figure when the Lord is ready to send me out then He will do so.

I asked the Lord once why I was not going out like I began, and he said, "If I want you to go to one person at a time, then you shall go to one person at a time." So I never asked again. And there is never a shortage of the "one person at a time." As a matter of fact, He keeps me rather busy.

But regardless, my life is much fuller, much richer as I serve the Lord every day. I have my Women On Fire For Christ ministry, and also a page on Facebook which is run by two of God's very faithful and awesome Women On Fire for the Lord, Alicia and Kathy! As my life is so full for my Lord, I am so thankful that He has given me associates for my ministry who love Him just as much as I do, and I leave most of it in their capable hands.

I also work full time with Bob in the summer in our business. But the funny thing is that many times I end up in ministry at the job site while Bob carries the work load. It is truly amazing where the Lord will place you to do His work and His will. As for Bob, he is still the Lord's angel, sent to be by my side through this entire journey until the trumpet blows.

18

My Dedication to My Dad

In October of 2014, I lost my dad to cancer. This was the person that I had originally signed up to help with Relay for Life for. My dad was actually only my stepfather, but he was more my father than any father I have ever known. He was there almost my entire life, and no matter how you look at it…he was my dad.

When he came down with cancer in the summer of 2013, I knew that we were going to lose him. Even though my family all kept trying to take him through the motions, I knew in my spirit that we were going to lose my dad. This summer, I was constantly flying back and forth with my grandson so I am grateful and I got to see quite a bit of him. By the time that I had to do the Relay for Life, my dad had gone quite a ways downhill.

Now, the real bad part!!! My dad was an atheist!!! I could never understand this when he was a firsthand witness to all of God's glory in my miracles. At least, let's just say he… said he was an atheist. But I think there was something deep down that my dad had anger over that he alone needed to get straight with the Lord Jesus. Maybe it was losing his dad on New Year's Eve to an automobile accident at a very young age, who knows? But anyway, I would constantly try to talk with Dad every time I went to Florida. Every time I went down, all he would say was "Yea, yea…" wave his hand, and you knew that he did not want to talk about it any more…

Then as He got sicker, I knew that he had not accepted the Lord yet, and I knew that we were getting ready to lose him. I was getting to desperation mode. I had my church praying, and I went to Florida a few more times and spoke to him a few more times. His response was always the same. Nothing!!! My last trip there I left very upset because I knew that unless we had a miracle that my dad was going to spend eternity in Hell. I loved my dad very much, and he truly was a good man. My heart was breaking, but I had no choice, I had to leave his bedside as I could not remain in Florida.

As I left Florida, I had one constant prayer to the Lord. "Lord, please give me a sign that he has accepted you if he does accept you before he dies." This was my constant prayer until the day he died. Well, that day came, as we knew it would in October of 2014. First of all, I had been praying to the Lord also to have him hang on until I had my church commitment completed before I had to leave to go north to the funeral. Well, it was the night of the church commitment, and I was finally done with it. I walked in the door that night, and my phone rang fifteen minutes later, telling me that Dad was breathing his last breaths. I was upset about Dad twofold, as I had not heard anything yet about if he had accepted the Lord, and that we would be losing our earthly dad. In the same breath, I was joyous that the Lord had honored my prayer to complete my commitment to him. He knew my heart and how vitally important this was for me. Joy and sorrow, what a combination!!!

The next morning, I got a phone call from both of my sisters, Debra and Barbara, who were by my dad's bedside the last days of his life. They both told me the same exact version of what they saw three days before my dad died. You see, my dad was so emancipated and the cancer had deteriorated his ability to speak so badly that for the last weeks of his life, he did not speak, nor was he able to move. But one night, just a few nights prior to his death, when everyone was there watching vigil, he let out a yell in the middle of the night.

They said everyone went running, as him making any noise was an unusual occurrence. Barbara, my sister, sat down on the side of the bed, and she said she thought it felt like there was someone there. The nurse who also just came into the room turned to her and said…That's nothing… look at his arms!!!

Barbara said when she turned around, his arms were not only straight up in the air, they looked like he was holding someone's hands. Both Barbara and Debra said the very same story.

For me, as soon as I heard this incredible story, it was enough for me. I knew that the Lord Jesus Himself had come for my dad. This was my sign that I had asked for at my dad's passing. People want to say angels, and some are saying a family member came to get Dad…no, I believe the Lord came and got him. But this does not end the story with my dad. It gets more phenomenal…watch!!!

If anyone did not know me, they would think that I was a fiction writer!!! But let me tell you, my friends, this has been my life, every single word of it!!! Now, Bob and I got into the car and headed to New Jersey to go to my dad's funeral. Yes, he lived in Florida, but he was buried in New Jersey. The rest of the family had already traveled in their cars from Florida to New Jersey. When we got there, I met up with our son, and then we went to meet up with my mom. It was the first time seeing her since Dad's passing. Why is it the truth that the only time families get together is for weddings and funerals?

My dad who loved family get-togethers would have loved his own funeral! I know I loved seeing people that I had not seen for many, many years…and then some!!! You see, when we were small children, we used to be real close with one set of our cousins. Our moms were both single moms and the cousins were always together. Altogether, there were eight of us. My mom had three girls, and my Aunt Sandra had four girls, Roberta, Marion, Stella, and Carol. Then she had one son, and his name is Robert. I tell you their names just to make telling this story easier.

It was almost at the beginning of the viewing when Roberta came up behind me and placed her hands on my eyes. For some reason, I knew who it was without even looking. It could have been ninety-nine people, but I knew it was Roberta, and I was right. I turned around and I saw all of them, with the exception of Carol. Wow, I had not seen them all in many years!!! I became so excited because behind her was Marion, and then behind her was Aunt Sandra, then Robert and then Stella. I went up to them all and gave each one of them a huge, and I do mean huge, hug. Even Robert gave me a great big bear hug!!! Everyone had something to say except Robert. He just smiled.

Now later in the service, I saw Carol walk in. I was speaking to my ex–brother-in -aw, and I asked to be excused because the "last of my cousins was here, and now they were all_here and I wanted to go say hi to her." So I politely excused myself and went over to Carol and gave her a great big hug also. I loved these guys so much as they represented a very large part of my very early years. It was so wonderful to see them all once again, my heart was full. I saw many people at my dad's funeral that I had just not seen in a very long time and had grown away from, yet I still love them dearly with all my heart. Like I said, it is sad that it takes weddings and funerals to bring those we love all together again.

After everything in my life so far, I did not think that the Lord could do too much more to blow my mind. Boy, was I wrong!!! Never underestimate the Lord!!! We were at the end of the viewing. I was sitting on the front row along the one side with my husband to one side of me and Roberta on my other side. Right in front of me was the podium for the speakers and to the right of that was my dad's casket. I forget why the topic came up, but Roberta and I were talking about speaking at the viewing.

Then Roberta says…Yes, when I did Robert's eulogy…"

God bless her she didn't get too far into that statement. For I was hitting her!!! I was also hitting Bob to the other side of me too! As a matter of fact, I was about to have a Holy Ghost fit right in the middle of my dad's viewing!!! I was just about speechless, but as I was hitting her, and I am hitting Bob, I am going, "No, you didn't do Robert's eulogy…you couldn't have done Robert's eulogy…you could not have done Robert's eulogy because he came in the door tonight right behind your mother!!! I even gave him a great big bear hug, and he gave me one back!!!"

Roberta turned to me and said, "You could not have given Robert a hug tonight…he died three years ago!"

I was doing everything but babbling by now!!! I could barely get anything out!!!

I told both Roberta and Bob. I said, "I am about ready to have a major Holy Ghost fit!!!" Roberta pointed to the podium and said, "There's the podium...go for it!!!"

It was now that Bob starts to chuckle...I hit him again... It's not funny!!!" But I think he knew what was going on before I did. As for me, I was so shaken that it took me a few minutes to gather my composure. I told you, this man has some major wisdom.

But Bob who knows how the windows of heaven have been opened for the past one year turned to me and said, "Ahah!!! So now we are entertaining angels, are we?" and he chuckles again. I truly did not think it was funny. I was not mad or anything. I think I was still amazed. I did not understand any of it yet, but I would very, very soon.

At my dad's viewing was Pastor Jim from North Carolina. He actually took the trip up to honor my dad also and to bring his son. He truly is an amazing man of God. I saw him on the other side of the room and made a mad dash for him. I told him what happened, and he just agreed with Bob basically. He said it was something to pray over, which knew I would be doing that. That was something that did not leave my mind for a long time. But I did not have to wait long, and my answer came the next morning.

Bob and I were staying in a hotel room in Flemington, New Jersey, as we were getting ready to go to my dad's funeral. As I stood in front of the mirror getting ready, I heard the Lord say very clearly to me six little words… **"Well, you asked for a sign!"**

I am telling you, one of these days, the Lord is going to make me poke myself in the eye as I am putting on my makeup! Again, he took me off guard, and I went running for Bob!!! I did not have to run far as we were in a motel room. But that was what He said, "Well, you asked for a sign!!!"

I knew immediately what He was talking about and to what He was referring to!!! I was like…yes, Lord, that was surely a sign!!!

Well, I can tell you this that I pondered that for many weeks. The meeting at the viewing was never far from my thoughts. Then one day, as I was meditating with the Lord, it was the Lord that told me to remember that even Mary Magdalene did not recognize Jesus after His resurrection. Jesus can change the way He looks. It was from this day forward that I truly believe that not only was that my sign that my dad is with Jesus in heaven, but my sign came directly from Jesus Himself!!! He walked into my dad's funeral, gave me a hug after all of these years away from Him (because I am so homesick!), and then He walked back out of my life!!! I look forward to the day soon when I shall be with Him forever, and I will never have to leave Him again.

Take care of my dad till we all get up there my wonderful, glorious Lord…Amen!

19

The Windows of Heaven

So here we are coming into 2015. It has now been over two full years since I have been healed from my Adhesive Arachnoiditis. I have been healed from two disintegrating knees. I have been given a brand-new spinal cord. I have been anointed into a Ministry for Evangelism by none other than the Lord God Almighty! I have been given the gift of healing for everyone that the Lord Jesus shall tell me…Pray for them." I am paying it forward! And I am now a mighty warrior with a total gift of spiritual warfare.

Let me tell you one more thing that began after my dad's funeral. Oh, Lord, I pray this one does not happen frequently, and as of yet, I am not totally comprehending the fullness of it. But I know the Lord is going to reveal it to me. When we got home from my dad's funeral, I began seeing what appeared to be demonic spirits going through my yard. They appeared to be circling my home. As I have said before, the demonic world does not intimidate me at all because I know what my power and authority is. I just did not understand the "why" of it, and I wanted to know why I was now able to see into the spiritual realm. God gave me the gift of spiritual warfare for a reason!

But let me tell you, they have sure been trying to pull down our stronghold! But remember earlier, I said they are dumb!!! Our Lord Jesus is mightier, stronger, more powerful, and shall defeat every one of them. I know that I have a job to do and no demonic trick, scheme, or ploy that they try shall stop me!!! As I said earlier, if they are taking the time to bother me, then they are leaving someone else alone! If they are so worried about me and my home and are trying to rip it down so mightily, then I just want to jump for joy!!! Thank you, Jesus, for your strength and your authority to put down the enemy that comes at me to lie, cheat, steal, and destroy!!! I know what I saw was the prelude to what came next over the next weeks. God gave me the blessing of being able to see that there were demonic spirits very heavily at work around my home. Not in my home, but just circling our property, ready for the attack!!!

I knew what we had done was the right thing, and every step that we took was the correct one. We stood for the Lord Jesus Christ, His precepts, His Word, and His moral code. So I know that we had this demonic world angry as a wild hornet!!! Our home, and Bob and I, in our lives, were not backing down. This is what is wrong with the world today. Everyone wants to live the "Happy Christianity," where it is all right to do as you please because everyone else is doing it. They then say it is all because this is why Jesus died on the cross, isn't it? Wow, have they missed the mark!!! This is a total other book, and I do not want to get into it here. You will find it in my Book of Bible Studies though. Look for Women on Fire for Christ Bible Studies I. Many of my studies speak of it. I am sorry, guys, you can not have your cake and eat it too. I will just say one thing here…Jesus told the woman at the well when He did forgive her…He told her…Now go…and sin no more." We are to turn from our sin.

But over two years ago, the Lord raised me from a bed that I was getting ready to go home again from, and this time, he opened up a direct line to Himself. I have not stopped talking to the Lord ever since that day. I have always heard the Lord, but ever since He got me up this time, it has been as if He moved in, bag and baggage. He says this time, we have a job to do and we are going forward!!! No enemy, no man, nobody is going to stop me. As the Lord opens those doors, I am walking through them... He says pray…I will pray…He says to go…I will go!!! I am His servant. I am no longer following man, I am following the Lord Jesus Christ and Him only. My shepherd is the Shepherd. I have totally surrendered my all, my everything to Him until that trumpet blows and we get to join Him in the air to follow Him to Glory!!!!!

I just want to make a note here that do I sit under pastors here that will be shepherds also of the Lord Jesus Christ? Yes, I will. Will I be an obedient servant within the walls of any church to which I follow? Yes, I will. With one exception. If they do not follow the Word of God or I see them being self-serving to themselves, I shall not serve a self-serving church. I serve a living God, and there is so very little time left, and the Lord is leading me and guiding me to where He alone wants me to be in these last hours to do the most good for the most people. For forty-five years, I did not know my mission for the Lord. I did not know my place. I just knew that at the age of ten years old, I sat at the feet of Jesus, and we talked together for a long time. I spent time with the King of the universe! This has kept me my entire life. Have I been longing to go home each time that I got so ill and bedridden? You are so right! When I knew I was terminal both times, I was happy. When the Lord did not take me home, I was sad. I was delirious that he had healed me, but not for the reasons that most would be happy. I was overjoyed because I knew of the testimony that would go forth for his glory. I did not care about my health nor that I was healed to be better. I just cared that the people would see God's glory each time that I was healed!!! Because personally, if we had our own choices, I would prefer to be home with my Jesus.

Now I know that as these days wane down and the sun is setting for all of God's children. The hour is drawing to a close. The Bridegroom is coming for His Bride at any given hour. If you read my Bible Studies, you shall read some of the Words that have been given by the Lord throughout this last year. The one given on December 24, 2014, was a mighty one. But yes, we are going home. Will you be ready? On March 8, 2014, I posted a Bible Study on My Facebook Ministry, Women on Fire for Christ, called "Have You Checked Your Oil Lately?" I believe that the Holy Spirit was mightily involved with the writing of that piece, just as He is with almost all of my Studies. You see I always know when it is me and when it is the Holy Spirit.

When I try to write something, I am constantly looking something up, backspacing, correcting, and erasing. When the Holy Spirit comes in to write a piece, it flows, and the writing is nonstop. That's what this book has been. I cannot believe how easy it has been to write this entire book. But I give all the glory to God. For it is the Lord God Almighty that has done all of these great things in my life, so that I can go forth with the testimony that I now have to take to others, and I can be a light shining in the darkness for the Lord. Jesus is our Light. He is our Lighthouse!!! Are you anchored by your lighthouse? If you came to our home, you would see two things. Lighthouses all over and wall-to-wall Thomas Kinkade. Why Thomas Kinkade? Number 1 because he was the painter of light!!! Number 2, if you know anything about him, he loved the Lord with all his heart. He is with the Lord as I sit here and write this. Lucky man! He also painted many beautiful lighthouses.

Is your light shining in the darkness? Is Jesus your lighthouse? Are you ready for the storms that are on the horizon? They are coming, my friend, and very soon. You could wake up and there may not be a tomorrow as you remember your yesterday to be. As these storms are raging and we are in the midst of the storms, Jesus is going to reach down His hands and pull us up out of the storms. He is your Lighthouse. Stay focused on that lighthouse, and keep your anchor holding!!!

God bless you all, my friends!!!

There is nothing, and I do mean nothing that God will not do for you!!!

> *But Jesus looked at them and said to them, "With men this is impossible, but with God all things are possible."*
>
> *(Matthew 19:26)*

Spiritual Warfare!!!
Don't Be Afraid of It !!!

Finally, my brethren, be strong in the Lord and in the power of His might. Put on the whole armor of God, that you may be able to stand against the wiles of the devil. For we do not wrestle against flesh and blood, but against principalities, against powers, against the rulers of the darkness of this age, against spiritual hosts of wickedness in the heavenly places. Therefore take up the whole armor of God, that you may be able to withstand in the evil day, and having done all, to stand.

Stand therefore, having girded your waist with truth, having put on the breastplate of righteousness, and having shod your feet with the preparation of the gospel of peace; above all, taking the shield of faith with which you will be able to quench all the fiery darts of the wicked one. And take the helmet of salvation, and the sword of the Spirit, which is the word of God; praying always with all prayer and supplication in the Spirit, being watchful to this end with all perseverance and supplication for all the saints—and for me, that utterance may be given to me, that I may open my mouth boldly to make known the mystery of the gospel, for which I am an ambassador in chains; that in it I may speak boldly, as I ought to speak. (Ephesians 6:10–20)

The above scripture has got to be the Lord's most famous scripture of all scripture for dealing with spiritual warfare. I think just about all true Christians have heard about the "armor." But what many pastors do not preach about is our power and authority. I have known about this all of my life. This is one place where I have never ever waivered. That is probably why the Lord has given me the mission he has now for going out in the battlefield to defeat the enemy. You see, as long as I have been exposed to the enemy, and as much battle as I have already been through, it was when the Lord revealed to me that it was the enemy that was taking me down that I was like that cat that hunched up its back and I got super mad!!! It was like, "Satan, look out now!!!"

Now please, no one ask me why it took me so long to find these things out, for I will have to wait until I see Jesus to get that answer! I guess I just had many lessons to learn along the way. Either that or I had to get as tough as I am today to go into the last battles that are up and coming in these following days just before He comes to get us. But one thing I know as an absolute, as sure as you know that you need air to breath…There is no power in Satan or his army that is taking me down again!!! I am up to stay…By the Lord's stripes, I am healed!!! That the enemy is a liar!!! He only comes to lie! Cheat! Steal! And destroy!!!

Now I know that if it is not something good coming down the pike, I go right after it and get it squashed right away! Even colds and sickness…usually!!! Sometimes one sneaks past, and I do end up with a cold. This is very rare. You should see my date book. If I have a cold coming on and I feel it, I go right after the demonic force that is bringing it on…I start rebuking it, saying…"Oh no, you don't!!!" and it immediately goes away. I log all of these into my date book!

Then I had a day recently where I was going ninety miles an hour doing something with the church. I was extremely busy, and I was just getting to the end of a twenty-one–day fast, which I already knew the enemy was in an uproar about that one! Well, I was going so fast and furious, and I felt my ear start hurting. Then my throat. Well, I did not stop to rebuke any demonic forces that day. I just did not take the time to stop and do it!!! By the next day, I was down big time!!! The immediate thing I was able to do was to rebuke the pain. I had such a bad ear infection, but no pain after I rebuked it!!! As I was going through a very rough time of it and the whole time rebuking the demonic forces that were trying to keep me down, I asked the Lord…"Lord, how did this happen? If we can move the mountains, then how did this one get in?"

I was taken back by the answer, but after I thought about it, I saw that it was 100 percent accurate…as the Lord always is!!!

He said, "You were going so hard, and not paying attention to yourself, that you allowed them to come in the backdoor!"

I was like…well, never again!!! I will stop take some time out and rebuke and renew myself to get anything off me just as I have been doing all along since I have learned how to do so! This will not happen again! If anyone sees me running fast and furious, shut me up in a closet or something! You see the enemy is very sly, and he even thought that I would break my fast the last three days by making some chicken soup and eating better just to feel better…wrong!!! I completed my fast for the Lord! Oh boy, do I know I had the enemy mad!!!

But let me share some things with you my friends, we do not need to be afraid of him. Do we need to be respectful of him? Oh yes, we most certainly do! Even Michael the Archangel had problems with Satan! (But of course, Michael won, just as we will always win!) But let me share some pertinent facts:

First of all for the most part, you are usually never dealing with Satan himself. You will have to be a pretty bigwig to do so. That boy has his hands full getting the Antichrist ready at the moment, and his home is in the Middle East. Or is it? That's what they say anyway. I have my doubts on some sides of that one.

Second…Satan is not Omnipresent. He cannot be in more than one place at a time. Neither can any of his little demonic minions! (That's what my favorite word is for his helpers.)

Third, he knows the Bible better than we do, and I do not care how well you know it!!! You had better remember

Satan has been around more than 6,000 years!!! Even into eternity past!!!

Fourth, he knows that his prophetic clock is at the midnight hour!!! He knows what is coming next. So he is not going to be wasting his time on those who are going to be following him into the lake of fire. He is going to go after the children of the Most High God.

Fifth, he is that roaring lion just as God says:

> *Be sober, be vigilant; because_your adversary the devil walks about like a roaring lion, seeking whom he may devour. (1 Peter 5:8)*

And when he can't get there, he sends his minions!!!

Sixth, these are the verses that the enemy hopes you will never see...

> *Behold, I give you the authority to trample on serpents and scorpions, and over all the power of the enemy, and nothing shall by any means hurt you. (Luke 10:19)*

> *Most assuredly, I say to you, he who believes in Me, the works that I do he will do also; and greater works than these he will do, because I go to My Father. And whatever you ask in My name, that I will do, that the Father may be glorified in the Son. If you ask anything in My name, I will do it. (John 14:12–14)*

Those are just a few items of fact for you to start with. The rest is that we have all the power and authority granted to us by the Lord Jesus Christ Himself to conquer and overrule anything that Satan or his minions send our way!!! There are so many scripture verses that tell us that if we just believe in Him and have faith in Him that we can have what we ask…We can move those mountains…God shall provide all of our need; as a matter of fact, he did not even say some…God said all!!!

Now I want to share with you something that happened the very beginning of my spiritual warfare ministry. I have a cousin in New Jersey. She has always been like my spiritual sister and my protégé. Yes, she has had her own issues, but she continuously tries to battle her way with the Lord. Her name is Sandy and she is a never-ending warrior in the ongoing battle for the Lord. Well, I know now that I taught her well how to be strong in the Lord when it comes to spiritual battles. I want to share her story because I believe it tells us in a nutshell the power and authority that we have over the spiritual world. Here is Sandy's story…

Sandy's Story

I had taught my cousin Sandy in New Jersey all about spiritual warfare before I left the north to come to North Carolina, but even after I got here, we continued with our teachings about the Lord. I sure wish I had her here now. We would sure make an awesome team! I want to share a story here about the power of knowing your power against the enemy! I did not know yet that the Lord was sending me in this direction, but I should have known when Sandy called early in 2013 that something was up. Sandy's little boy, Bradon, who was about eight, who has a touch of autism, was hearing demonic voices. These voices were telling him to burn down their home. They were trying everything to get him help. They even had him committed to a hospital. Nothing was working.

Sandy and I both knew what it was, and we both knew what needed to be done. I kept telling Sandy to call the pastor. She had just begun going to a new church. Well, this pastor did not want to answer her call. I even tried calling and emailing from here in North Carolina. I urgently tried reaching him, I did not want this girl going against this demonic force alone! Boy...let me tell you what: I was not a happy camper with this pastor!!!

You just have to love some of our pastors these days! So as a few weeks went by and she kept trying to deal with the situation by herself, and she was praying on her end, Bob, I, and our church with Pastor Jim and Bea were praying on this end constantly for this situation, he just kept getting worse, and the voices were getting stronger, and the things that he was being told to do were becoming more violent. She could still not get a response from her pastor!!!

They finally released him from the hospital, and as of yet, nothing had been done for him. But we knew what needed to be done, I just did not want her alone in this. One day, she took her two children out to dinner. She also had an older daughter, about twelve years old, Hailey. As Sandy was on her way home and things were getting bad, she said, "That's it, kids, we are taking care of this situation…right now!!!" As she was going home, Bob and I were praying mightily!!!

I know Bob's prayer was for the Lord to place his angels at all four corners of that home that night…I can never forget it because of the events that were happening…

She proceeded to drive directly home, and she took her two small children into her living room where her windows were open because it was springtime. They stood in the middle of the living room floor in a circle, and Sandy began to pray hard and to rebuke any and all the demonic forces that were attacking her child!!! You would have to know this woman and how she is with her children! I can just imagine the fierceness of her prayers!!! Sandy kept praying and praying until the child said that the demon was gone. Bradon said, "Mom, the demon flew out the window!!!" He actually saw the demon fly out of the open window! But as he was talking, he said to his mom, "Mom, there is another one…" This little boy had some gifts of his own!!!

Mom says, "Oh no, you don't!!!" So here Sandy starts again!!! She begins again to rebuke and to chase out every demonic force that is within her child! Finally, the demonic force is freed from her beloved Bradon, and he is free from all demons that has been tormenting him for weeks on end.

Even to the point of a mental hospital, believe me, that was a scary situation!!!

Now, as Mom is totally wiped out and drained as you can well imagine...The daughter Hailey is looking at Mom, just wide eyed and stunned...but it was her son that gives her the best surprise of all...

He said..."Mom, when you were praying, Jesus was standing in the middle of us."

I think Sandy lost it just about then...Her praise and glory totally went to the Lord Jesus Christ for all that He did.

So here is a Mom that could get no help from the church, and I can tell you, I was just about to fly up from North Carolina to help her, and she decided to go at it herself. Now this is not something I recommend to anyone! This kind of spiritual warfare is very serious. To do what she did takes someone that has a very strong and determined spirit. This is why I wish she lived here. We would be one powerhouse team! I taught that girl all I know about spiritual warfare. And when she could get no help, she got the King of the universe Himself!!! She trusts the Lord with all her heart. This is faith!!!

> *For where two or three are gathered together in My name, I am there in the midst of them. (Matthew 18:20)*

Do you see how true God's Word is? Bradon, this child that is slightly autistic, not only saw the demons as they left, he saw Jesus as He stood in the center of them all. Now just how glorious and how wonderful is all of that!!! I am telling you though, He came down to protect her!!! Because she had gone somewhere that she probably should not have gone alone! Even Jesus sent out His disciples in pairs everywhere they went. Even to go get a donkey!!! So you see we have the power and the authority, but always do it as you should and always be well schooled in spiritual warfare before doing anything like this one.

But standing up to the wiles of the evil one...you can do so every day!!! Just praise Jesus!!! Worship Jesus!!! Proclaim His name, and stand for Him, and you shall not fall!!!

◆

Since all of this has happened this last time, I know one thing, and that is that I have become a major mountain mover...I refuse, and I do mean refuse, to allow the lies that the enemy tries to tell us that we cannot do this, or we cannot serve there to penetrate any where within the vicinity of my life!!! I am a child of the King of Glory, and I have a job and a testimony to get out to those whom the Lord will have me to tell. No demonic power or no enemy of my God shall keep me from going forth.

Now, my friends, you just stop and think...what kind of last hour would we have for the Lord's Army to get out there and reap His harvest if we all could have this kind of attitude, and we all had this kind of courage to face the enemy dead on and say, "You cannot defeat me anymore!!!" We would have an army on the march that could not be stopped, we could not be put down, and we would reap a harvest that would be so glorious that when that trumpet blows, this earth would look barren!!! Wow, that sure does sound wonderful, doesn't it?

Unfortunately, I know we have too many still in boot camp that are still in training and are still afraid of the adversary and afraid to go to war. But they better pull themselves up by their bootstraps, get their armor in place if they want to be a child of God, because the war is just over the next hill. Then we are racing to the finish line, and our part of that battle will be over!!! I for one want to take as many with me as I can. For those whom are left behind, it shall be such devastation and such carnage that this world cannot even fathom, and such as it has never seen before. I pray you are not here to see any of it, may God bring you home on the first load as His Bride.

Ouch...another rabbit trail...I have a bad habit of doing that. Half the time I do not know if it is me or if the Holy Spirit wants to go in another direction. I do know that the point I am trying to make in all of this is to stand up to the enemy. Even though he is a tough adversary, you are tougher...Some days we may not feel so, and when the enemy is pounding real hard is when we least feel like we have the power over the enemy. This is when all you need to do is to cry out…Jesus!!!" Just keep crying out His name, for the Lord God knows your needs even before you ask them and those demonic forces that are trying to destroy you must…oh, my friend, let me repeat…must flee!!!

Now as I tell you all of this, I hope that everyone understands that when you do any of these things they truly must be coming from your heart to the living God. For the Lord does not want lip service. Oh, so many people try to defeat the enemy and say…"Well, I cry out to Jesus, but He doesn't hear me, and the enemy keeps beating me up." This same person goes to bars on the weekend, or still continues to get drunk at night, you see them using foul language to their friends…oh yes, once in a while, they post a Christian quote, but for the most part, you need to delete their posts so no one sees the foul language on your page. These same people say…"But why doesn't God answer my prayers?"

Many of these people are living in Satan's world, and God is going to leave them there wallowing in the muck and the mire until they fully come to their senses and come out of the pigpen and come home. This is why Jesus gave us the parable of the prodigal son. He knew that Satan was going to come and to pull His children off into the sin of this world. Now once off in this sinful world…you have two choices just as the prodigal son did. You can struggle with having little to eat and feeding the pigs for someone else…or you can leave Satan's world and go home to your

Father and repent of your sins. The parable that Jesus told goes on to say that the father of the son actually met the son on the way back home. He saw the son coming and went out to meet him. Then the father was so happy that he gave him the best robe, the best ring, and a fatted calf and threw him a party (Luke 15:11–32).

God's Word tells us that there is more joy in heaven over one sinner who repents than ninety-nine just persons who need no repentance (Luke 15:7).

So you see, if you turn back from that pigpen which is called your world…and repent and come back to the Lord Jesus Christ, He is waiting for you, and He will even meet you on the way! But God cannot look upon sin, and He sent His one and only son to a cross two thousand years ago to suffer and die for each and every one of us. Not one of us deserved not one second of the suffering that was inflicted upon this man that went to Calvary in *our place*. We are the sinners!!! He had no sin!!! But He took on our sin, so that we would never have to pay any penalty for the sins that we have done in this lifetime. I can not even begin to fathom or imagine the unending love that comes from a man that can make such a sacrifice for an entire world for that day and for all eternity. There is no other man, other than the Son of the Almighty God…Jesus Christ, who could and did do such a thing for you and for me!!!

Now He has only asked one thing from us in return, and that is our belief in Him. Our love for Him in return. Wow,

I know I love Him with my whole entire being. He asks us to repent from our sins and to turn to Him, so that He can wash us clean with the blood that He shed at Calvary. He will take His own Blood and use it to wipe away every one of your sins for all eternity. All you need to do is to ask.

One of the most famous pieces of scripture says…

> **For God so loved the world that He gave His only Begotten Son, that whosoever believeth in Him shall not perish, but have everlasting life. (John 3:16)**

If you would like to belong to the King of kings and Lord of lords or if you just need to get back to where you once were with Him, you can just ask the Lord to forgive your sins today and wash you clean…

Say, "…Lord Jesus, I know that you died on the cross for my sins, and I believe with all of my heart that you love me too and I love you with all of my heart and all of my mind and soul. Lord, please forgive me of my sins and wash me white as snow as your Word says I can be, as I choose to forever belong to you, now and for all eternity. Amen."

Now I know it is not the fanciest of sinner's prayers, but our Lord Jesus knows and hears your heart. He is not judging your vocabulary, nor your eloquence. He is looking at your sincerity and your heart. I pray that if you have made a decision for Christ that you will either contact myself, which I will have contact information at the end of this book, or please get in contact with your local church and speak to the pastor, and by all means, begin to attend church.

For I can assure you of one thing…the very thing you just did, the enemy is going to come in and seek to destroy. You are going to need some help. Please do not feel like you do not need the help because you do!!! You are what the Lord calls in His Word, just a baby in Christ, and they are the weakest that the enemy can devour. There are plenty of people at your local church that can help you get learned and knowledgeable into knowing how to stand firm. But the very first thing is to read God's Word!!! If you do not have that, you let me know, we will make sure that you get His Word into your hands, if you have indeed made a decision for Christ!!!

I pray that each and every person that has taken the time to read this book shall be blessed with many blessings as I know that the testimonies that the Lord has given me to proclaim to the world for Him are for Him and His glory, and if I can just take one person more to glory with me, then praise be to God, then maybe I have done something.

> *Therefore submit to God. Resist the devil and he will flee from you. (James 4:7)*

God bless you all!
Maranatha.
Mary

For additional copies of this book please contact me at:

Womenonfire4Christ@gmail.com

You can also visit our Facebook page at:

Women on Fire for Christ

For your encouraging Word for the day…Kathy and Alicia are constantly sharing God's encouraging Word for our daily lives and even our daily struggles. God always has the right word for the right time

And last but most important…if you have made a decision to follow the Lord Jesus Christ during the reading of this book or even just recently in your life, we would like to help you at Women on Fire to grow in the Word of God and to help you become a stronger child of the King. If you need a Bible or if you need someone to help you to understand God's Word, please feel free to contact us at the above e-mail address. It is our constant mission and endeavor to minister to those who are in the kingdom of the Living God and to get them home safely.

I will respond to each e-mail personally and each need shall be addressed as the Lord shall direct. For He alone is our provider and He shall provide all of my needs and all of your needs! But I want everyone to be equipped with God's Word, so please contact me especially if you need a Bible.

God bless and keep you all!

Maranatha